The Grand Masters of
Maine
Gardening

Hot pink phlox and 'Basket of Gold' alyssum combine for an exuberant groundcover.

The Grand Masters of
Maine
Gardening
And Some of
Their Disciples

Jane Lamb

Copyright © 2004 by Jane W. Lamb
ISBN 0-89272-637-7
LCCN: 2003113980
Printed in China
RPS

5 4 3 2 1

Down East Books
A division of Down East Enterprise, Inc.,
Publisher of *Down East*, the Magazine of Maine

Book orders: 1-800-685-7962
www.downeastbooks.com

The profiles in this book were first published, in slightly different form, as articles in *Down East* magazine. Dates and original titles are listed below. All articles © by Jane W. Lamb.

Asticou, a Beatrix Farrand Legacy (May 1990, "Asticou")
Bare Ledge Blossoms for Phid and Sharon Lawless (July 2000, "The Quarry Garden")
Beatrix Farrand and Betsy Moore, Master Designer and Disciple (August 1989, "Keeper of the Flame")
Bernard Etzel, Farmington's Master Gardener (August 1996, "A Passion for Color")
Bernard McLaughlin, Dean of Maine Gardeners (July 1986, "Fifty Years a Gardener")
Carolyn Jenson, Sod-Top Gardener (February 1993, "Islands of Color")
Celia Thaxter's Victorian Garden (August 1986, "Hollyhocks, Poppies, and Sweet Peas")
Charles Savage's Thuya Garden (February 1994, "The Secret Garden")
Corinne Mann's Daylilies (August 1984, "The Daylily Lady of Kittery Point")
The Cottage Garden (March 1991, "A Maine Cottage Garden")
Currier McEwen, World-Famous Iris Hybridizer (May 1982, "The Importance of Being Tetraploid")
Debbie Deal's Delphiniums (February 1997, "Do-It-Yourself Delphiniums")
Doc Pinfold's Daffodils—and Lupines (May 1998, "Afloat in a Sea of Daffodils")
A Gardening Heritage Lives On in Kezar Falls (July 2001, "An Heirloom Garden")
Five Hundred Enchanting Irises (June 1986, "How's This For a Backyard?")
Heather Blooms at High Tide (October 1992, "The Heathers of October")
Lupines on the Front Lawn, Birds in the Bush (February 1995, "A Wildflower Lawn")
Maine's Rare Wild Rhododendrons (July 1992, "Last of the Great Laurels")
Nellie Davis Stops Traffic at Bean's Corner (August 1998, "The Lord and Nellie")
Old Sheep Meadows Grows Roses for Maine (August, 2003, "Maine-Hardy Roses")
Patrick Chassé Designs a Garden for Mainers (February 1992, "An Ideal Maine Garden")
Roger Luce, Maine's Dean of Magnolias (May 2003, "Magnolias in Maine?")
The Sawyers Light Up the Shade (April 2001, "Shade Lovers")
Tom York's Rhododendrons (May 2000, "Survival of the Fittest")
Wild Asters, Beautiful and Bountiful (September 1991, "Asters")
Wild Roses for the Garden (June 1993, "Coming Up Roses")

To my mother, Edna Wallace,
who taught me the love of gardening,
and my daughter, Lucinda Clark,
who keeps the faith

In memory of the Grand Masters of Maine Gardening: Currier McEwen, Bernard McLaughlin, and Roger Luce

Contents

Acknowledgments

I wish to thank the gardeners profiled in this book, as well as all the others I met who, with their enthusiasm and generosity, made garden writing such a joy; Dale Kuhnert, editor of *Down East* magazine, who kept me seeking great gardens and great gardeners year after year; Karin Womer, Senior Editor at Down East Books, whose idea it was to put that experience into a book; Rick Sawyer for his help with the Roger Luce story; Patrick Chassé, for his generous assistance with Beatrix Farrand material and his horticultural acumen; my grandchildren, Aurora Clark-Grohman and Owen Grohman, for their invaluable computer expertise; and my family and friends, who cheered me on.

Introduction

For more than twenty years, I have had the privilege of meeting dozens of Maine gardeners in the course of writing about them for *Down East* magazine. Each of them has added something new and stimulating to my own gardening experience as well as to that of the many readers who have responded to the articles. I have had the joy of visiting more beautiful displays of flowers and trees than I had dreamed possible in Maine's challenging climate. Best of all, I have had the honor of meeting some of the horticultural pioneers who dared to test the limits of "what will grow in Maine" and to go beyond them with amazing success. These are the "grand masters": the late Dr. Currier McEwen, internationally known hybridizer of Siberian and Japanese irises, who was still directing his garden's progress at age 102; the late Bernard McLaughlin, "Dean of Maine Gardeners," whose renowned perennial garden in South Paris has been preserved by the McLaughlin Foundation; and Roger Luce, "Maine's Dean of Magnolias," who died in November 2002 at the age of 82, leaving behind a remarkable horticultural legacy.

Their disciples are numerous, and many qualify as "deans" themselves. In Maine's congenial statewide neighborhood, most of them are acquainted with one another. They often share information, advice, and plant material. A common interest among them is Maine's ecology and natural landscape, which leads to some ingenious adaptations of terrain and soil conditions. Wildflowers blend with old favorites in Maine's predominantly informal setting, resulting in a wide variety of "cottage gardens," whether by design or accident. What make this fellowship of Maine gardeners so fruitful are the many connections among them. Whether they are reserved or voluble, they are all fascinating individuals, and their enthusiasm for gardening is contagious. Their generosity with information has inspired hundreds of readers and provided them with the how-to details to realize their dreams.

The following chapters were originally published as articles in *Down East* magazine from 1982 to 2003. Updated information, as of July 2003, appears in the brief introduction to each chapter. —J. L.

Currier McEwen,
World-Famous Iris Hybridizer

Currier McEwen was the first gardener I interviewed for Down East, *in 1982. Twenty years later, I visited him and Elisabeth in the same sunny family room overlooking the sea, and he was as exuberant as ever. He was still hybridizing irises, though now from his car, driven as close to the garden as possible, where he could give directions to his longtime assistant, Sharon Hayes Whitney. "I'm introducing two this year," he told me in his hearty voice. "'Little Centennial', a diploid Siberian, and 'Centenary', a magnificent purple tetraploid Japanese. There will be more." His formula for longevity: "Always have a new goal."*

Currier McEwen celebrated his hundred and second birthday April 1, 2003. He was still driving his own car a few weeks before his death on June 23. His family reports him saying often in his last days, "I've had a wonderful life. I'm a very lucky man."

If you're looking for Currier McEwen anytime but midwinter, chances are you'll find him in one of the gardens at his South Harpswell home—that is, if he's not out of town for a medical or horticultural meeting, or at the hospital in Brunswick attending patients, or off to the Scottish Highlands or the Isles of Greece with his new bride. At an age when most men of his accomplishments are content to rest upon their laurels, eighty-year-old Dr. Currier McEwen still finds twenty-four hours too short a day for his twin passions, flowers and arthritis. More specifically, Dr. McEwen is one of the world's foremost hybridizers of irises and a nationally recognized rheumatologist.

In May, he's especially likely to be around his home, up with the sun to savor the scent of spring bulbs on the salt air and to keep a close check on the early dwarf irises that come into bloom toward the end of the month. And in June and July, when his world-renowned Siberian and Japanese irises crown the sunny slope above Harpswell Sound with their broad splashes of blue and white, their rarer accents of yellow and red and pale green, you won't find him anywhere else. Literally busy as a bee, he'll be engrossed in beating nature's haphazard geneticists to the draw, cross-pollinating selected specimens, tying up and tagging blossoms, recording his experiments, and dreaming on the possibilities of a true blue or a pure pink.

McEwen's gardens, protected from the ceaseless sea winds by the wild rose thicket from which they were carved, command a matchless view of Orrs and Bailey Islands and the Gulf of Maine to the east and the Casco Bay archipelago to the south. It was there that I first met him.

His tall, angular figure, as he moves to greet a visitor with a purposeful lope across the carefully groomed rows of Siberian iris, is as vigorous and enduring as the setting. The cordially twinkling blue eyes behind the square tortoiseshell glasses, the white hair that must once have been sandy ruffling in the breeze, the firm handshake are complemented

by the sparkling water beyond, the unseason-
ably warm sun above, and the stalwart bedrock
beneath. Yet there is a cosmopolitan ease
about him that suggests McEwen is equally at
home in New York or Tokyo.

Relaxing later in the sun-drenched family
room that overlooks the gardens and shares
their prospect of sea and sky, I learn how
McEwen, a pioneer in arthritis research who
still puts in two days a week as a consulting
rheumatologist, got to be the world's leading
hybridizer of Siberian and Japanese irises.

"I can say with small modesty"—and he
smiles disarmingly—"that I'm the biggest hybridizer of Siberian irises in the world. I make
more crosses and put in more seedlings each
year than anyone else. It's beginning to catch
on in England and West Germany."

Until he was into his fifties, McEwen had
no interest whatever in gardening. Harpswell,
where he had spent every summer since 1902
except for the war years, was for sailing,
tennis, family fun. Then in 1956, the postman
left a catalog from Schreiner's Iris Gardens
(Salem, Oregon) at his New York home.

"It wasn't for us, and I tried to give it
back," he recalls, "but the postman said there
was no such address and since it was for a Mc-
somebody, we should keep it. One cold winter
day I opened it. It was full of lovely colored
pictures, and it was just the right time of year
for it. I put in an order. I planted my first iris
in 1956 and made my first crosses in 1957.
When I do things, I do them whole hog."

He joined the American Iris Society and
was captivated by an article on hybridization
in its bulletin. He went to see the author to
learn how it was done. Later, at a medical
meeting in Chicago, he heard that living
nearby was Orville Fay, one of the greatest
figures in hybridizing daylilies and tall
bearded iris. Without delay he visited the

*Currier McEwen started gardening almost
by accident in 1956 and spent the next
forty-five years developing spectacular new
iris hybrids.*

man, who showed him experiments with
growing lights and, much more exciting to
McEwen's scientific mind, his work with
colchicine.

Colchicine is a drug obtained from the
autumn crocus that has been used for centuries in the treatment of gout, a coincidental
connection with McEwen's arthritis studies. It
can also cause the doubling of chromosomes
in certain plants. McEwen, whose perspica-
cious eye no sooner lights on a new field of
inquiry than he is exploring its frontiers, was
enchanted.

"I started gardening with daylilies and tall
bearded iris, but I switched my love to
Siberians for two reasons. First, the tall

Merriconeag Sound and Bailey Island in the distance are a breathtaking backdrop for McEwen's famed garden.

beardeds are susceptible to many diseases, which makes them a nuisance. But the principal reason was my interest in using colchicine." He is now equally interested in Japanese irises.

Siberian irises, he explains, have two sets of chromosomes, fourteen from each parent, to make twenty-eight in each cell. They are called diploid, or twofold. Sometimes plants spontaneously double their chromosomes to become tetraploid, or fourfold. A tetraploid Siberian, for example, would have fifty-six chromosomes. This had occurred in nature with tall bearded irises but never with Siberian or Japanese. Here was the challenge.

"The excitement of hybridizing is to get something new," McEwen confesses. "The most exciting thing was to develop tetraploids in Siberian and Japanese irises. I was the first to do it," he says, beaming. "It's always better to be tetraploid than diploid. Tetraploids are bigger, showier, more stalwart. Diploids are dainty, dear things. I introduce some of each every year." Indeed, one of his most important breakthroughs was a diploid, 'Butter and Sugar', the first yellow twenty-eight chromosome Siberian iris.

McEwen began experimenting with colchicine in 1962, but wasn't successful in getting a second-generation tetraploid until 1968. "It was pure chance. I got a blue tetraploid and named it 'Orville Fay' for the man who taught me how to do it." 'Orville Fay' was introduced to the market in 1970 and won the Morgan Award of the Society of Siberian Irises in 1976. Since then, McEwen has won that award and others nearly every year.

There are two ways of treating a plant with colchicine to try to induce the doubling of chromosomes. One is to cut the stem of a year-old plant about an inch above the crown, scoop out a tiny cup, and drop in some colchicine; the other is to treat the sprouted seeds with the same solution. The effect of colchicine is to interrupt temporarily the normal cell division in plant growth.

"When it wears off, the chromosomes go on dividing as usual ninety percent of the time. But about ten percent of them get so confused they forget they have already divided and do it again. Each daughter cell has twice the number of chromosomes and goes on dividing forever with double the number.

"When you treat a hundred seedlings with colchicine, most will die. Of those that survive, most won't change. Only one or two might be tetraploid, and some of these will be only half changed. They're called chimeras. Not until the second generation can you be sure you have a pure tetraploid. You can reproduce these indefinitely by dividing the plants."

The specimens McEwen chooses to name, register and introduce are propagated in sufficient numbers for the market by dividing clumps, or cloning, the only way to get identical plants. These are raised in a large "selling bed." There's also a display garden, visited by hundreds of people every summer. For many years, McEwen put out two thousand to four thousand Siberian and Japanese seedlings each year. Now, because he is refining his technique, it's down to about fifteen hundred. Of these he selects a maximum of ten for naming.

The rest he gives away. "They're new, but not named, and most are better than any that can be bought," he says.

Meanwhile the process of hybridization goes on. Because he wants to be sure he's crossing tetraploids, he takes his microscope into the garden and examines the pollen grains of desirable blooms. A tetraploid grain has about twice the volume of a diploid grain. A measuring device in the eyepiece of the microscope verifies his experienced judgment.

The fun of hybridization, says McEwen, is to try to breed for certain characteristics in much the same manner as selective breeding of animals. "I'm after a green," he confides. "'Dreaming Green' is white with a lot of green lines. I'm also after a pink and a true blue. Some irises look blue until you hold them against a delphinium."

Aside from color there are several other sought-after characteristics. "Dr. McEwen is putting texture into Japanese irises they never had before," says Shirley Pope of Gorham, a past president of the Maine Iris Society. "Dinner-plate-size Japanese can be very floppy. He's making them as sturdy as gardenias." Mrs. Pope is a staunch McEwen fan, and he has returned the compliment by naming a handsome deep purple Siberian after her.

"She's one of the dearest women," he remarks. McEwen's love of flowers reflects his even warmer regard for people. Some of his favorite irises are named after his favorite people, among them, his fellow masters, Bernard McLaughlin and Roger Luce. 'Dear Delight', a charming light blue tetraploid, is named after his first wife, Kay, who died in a tragic automobile accident in 1980. 'Dear Dianne', a silver-edged purple, is named for his daughter-in-law; 'Ewen', his first tetraploid red, for his son, Ewen McEwen. "Yes, that's his name. It's rather precious, isn't it?" he admits with a hint of self-deprecation.

Ewen, a doctor like his father, lives in Cleveland but visits Harpswell every summer. Last year, daughter Kathy and her husband, Hubbard Goodrich, with their children Kaline and Kevin, returned home after nine years in Saudi Arabia, where she was a nurse and he a teacher. Two other daughters are teachers, Ann in Saudi Arabia and Tillie in New York. Altogether, there are six grandchildren.

"Everyone comes here every summer. We always have. That's one of the advantages of teaching jobs. We have a wonderful time. They all love the place as much as I do. Fortunately for me, the iris love it here, too. They need a cold winter. They're not so happy in the South.

"I've been coming here since I was three months old. My grandfather Osceola Currier was one of the founders of the so-called Auburn Colony of summer cottages here in South Harpswell, the only one not from Auburn. He was from Newark, New Jersey, and was named after the Seminole chief who carried on a guerrilla war with the United States for years. When Osceola came out of the swamp under a flag of truce [and was] taken prisoner and executed, my great-grand-father Cyrus Currier, originally of Amesbury, Massachusetts, was incensed. He named his son Osceola in his honor. My first name is Osceola, but I don't use it." The McEwen sailboat, a Small Point day sailer now used mostly by the younger generation, is the *Seminole*, however.

Currier McEwen was born in Newark, where his father was a surgeon. Crippled by

"Tetraploids are bigger, showier, more stalwart. Diploids are dainty, dear things."

arthritis, the elder McEwen gave up surgery and became a pediatrician. He designed a table for examining a child on his lap, because he was unable to move from his chair. "He had an elevator from his office to his bedroom above and lived between the two for years. He kept up his practice and put two children through college," his son relates with understandable pride.

McEwen graduated from Wesleyan College in Middle-town, Connecticut, and in 1926 from New York University (NYU) School of Medicine. "When I graduated from medical school, arthritis was the for-gotten disease of medicine," he notes. "There was no academic department in the country com-parable to those that were taken for granted in other diseases." Motivated by his father's affliction and his own love of chal-lenge, he plunged into the void. After in-terning at Bellevue Hospital, he went to the Rockefeller Institute for four years of research in rheumatoid diseases. He returned to NYU as an instructor in medicine and served as dean there for eighteen years. During World War II he was the U.S. Army's chief counselor in medicine for the European theater.

"After the war, I'd had enough of adminis-tration. I resigned as dean and stayed in rheumatic diseases," he continues. He had founded the arthritis unit at NYU in 1932, the third in the country. A fourth was established in 1939, then no more for years. McEwen was instrumental in making a new start in 1960. As a member of the council of the National Insti-tute of Arthritic and Metabolic Diseases and chairman of its project committee, he lobbied for congressional money to support big re-search projects and also raised funds through the National Arthritis Foundation, of which he was a founder.

"Now there's hardly a medical school in the country that doesn't take a deep interest in arthritis," he states with satisfaction. "My chief role has been to define the different types of arthritis." Having been identified as separate diseases, these can now be treated more successfully, he says. Major areas of improvement have been in the control of rheumatic fever and gout, and the cure of bacterial diseases of the joints with antibiotics. McEwen has been responsible for separating rheumatoid arthritis, the most devastating form, from gout and from osteoarthritis, the common type associated with aging, and in pinpointing psoriatic arthritis, which attacked his father.

When he retired in 1970 and moved to Harpswell permanently, McEwen planned to devote full time to gardening. "But that's impossible when you're a specialist in an under-supplied field," he smiles. "At that time, there were only three rheumatologists in the state, all in Portland. Now there are twelve. My medical friends in Brunswick asked me to see an occasional patient, and I've been at it ever since."

He organized the Maine Chapter of the National Arthritis Foundation and a program of consulting visits throughout the state. For three years he and Kay made monthly trips to twelve hospitals from Lewiston to Fort Kent. It was on one of these trips that Kay was fatally injured. McEwen was also hurt in the collision, but not seriously. He made his last trip to Fort Kent a year ago. Now northern Maine is served by Bangor rheumatologists, but he still has office hours in Brunswick twice a week and visits the veterans' hospital at Togus once a month.

The sun has set over Potts Point at the tip of Harpswell Neck. Halfway Rock, on the

LYNN KARLIN

'Dear Dianne', one of Currier McEwen's many iris cultivars.

southern horizon, is winking its five-second flash. Daughter Kathy comes in with a tray of snacks. McEwen is telling me how the family bought the house, then a summer cottage, in 1952. "We added this big wing in 1968. The children and I had the most wonderful time planning and building it. I found this book in the Grand Central Station bookstore: *Your Dream House: How to Build It for Less*, for $3.98. The best investment I ever made!"

"You say that twice a day," Kathy teases.

The rest of the family drifts in and McEwen takes orders for drinks. We join in a toast: "To Mother!"

"Daffodils were her favorite flower," McEwen observes appreciatively, comfortable with her memory. "Hubbard and Kathy have planted bunches of them. I was going to try hybridizing them, but when I learned it took six years from seed to blossom, I decided it wasn't a very promising project at age eighty." A practical but hardly dreary consideration for a man who has just turned over all the shipping and selling aspects of his iris business to neighbor and fellow hybridizer Howard Brooks in order to have plenty of time to travel with Elisabeth, the family friend of thirty-five years who became the new Mrs. McEwen just last January.

"If he weren't such a special man, I never would have married him," says the bride, who, at sixty-nine, enjoys trying to keep pace with her peripatetic husband. "He combines so much strength with so much gentleness. He's also lots of fun."

McEwen calls his iris enterprise his creative outlet. "Most everybody has a wish to be creative. I don't play anything or paint. This is my form of expression. But I don't have as much energy as I used to. I work ten hours a day, but now I can only write letters after dinner. More serious things make me too sleepy."

McEwen is currently engaged in writing a history of arthritis research with two other rheumatologists. He is also the author of technical papers and articles on iris culture and recently wrote a book on the subject for the Society of Siberian Irises, of which he is a director and active committee member. He belongs to Siberian iris societies in Canada and Japan, attends national and international conventions, and corresponds with and visits iris growers everywhere.

"I have friends all over the world," he acknowledges happily. "That's the nicest thing about working with flowers or arthritis." Nevertheless, when queried about the scene of the most exciting iris activity in the world, he answers without hesitation: "Quite frankly, right here!"

Bernard McLaughlin,
Dean of Maine Gardeners

Not only the gardeners appearing in this book but others all over the state have paid tribute to Bernard McLaughlin. Most have visited his South Paris gardens, and many were his good friends. Bernard McLaughlin died in 1995 at the age of ninety-eight, a decade after I had interviewed him for this profile. His gardens and historic farmhouse and barn have been preserved by the McLaughlin Foundation, established in 1996. The gardens are open to visitors daily during the season. The McLaughlin Garden and Horticultural Center, now marked with a distinctive sign, is open year-round for classes, lectures, and workshops. Fourteen thousand visitors made the pilgrimage to the center in 2002, and it was voted "Favorite Public Garden in New England" for four years running in the People, Places, and Plants *readership poll.*

Anyone looking for the man who has been called the "Dean of Maine gardeners"—and his garden— would have trouble finding him without specific directions. Bernard McLaughlin's well-kept, two-story, nineteenth-century farmhouse is one of the few remaining survivors of an earlier era among the filling stations, fast food stops, and shopping plazas on South Paris's Main Street. The house stands quietly behind its screen of evergreens, reserved but by no means forbidding. You just have to know that this really *is* the driveway to turn into—"just before the second railroad"— to find one of the state's outstanding gardens.

If you arrive anytime between April and November, don't bother to knock on the door. Just follow the tree-shaded path around the barn. Somewhere among the irises or lilacs, the lilies or hostas, depending on the season, you will probably find McLaughlin, planting a new acquisition or administering tender loving care to a long-cherished specimen. If he's not around, he's likely attending a garden meeting somewhere, but you're welcome to look. And even if he's there, after a cordial greeting he may invite you to be your own guide and come back to him with any questions after you've completed your tour. With nearly two thousand visitors in a season, some coming in busloads, he can accompany only those who have made special arrangements.

What brings these multitudes to South Paris is not a spectacular display of color or an example of elaborate landscape design but a collection of perennials, shrubs, and trees assembled with love and discrimination, established in a natural setting, and assiduously nurtured for fifty years.

Bernard McLaughlin (never "Bernie," even to his closest friends, whose affectionate respect for this gracious man precludes any presumptuous familiarity) turned eighty-eight years old in February. He shares with his garden a quiet reserve that conceals a rich diversity. A glow of warm appreciation when he speaks of a particular flower or friend, a small chuckle seasoning a gardening anecdote, a sudden outburst of

More than fifty years ago Bernard McLaughlin planted the pasture around his house with the trees that now dapple his garden with pleasant shade.

sheer delight as he looks up from a plant he's discussing: "Isn't the sky handsome! Look at those clouds"—all illuminate his gentle dignity like the sunlight that dapples his woodland path or the sparks of brilliant bloom along his garden's cool, green alleys.

The longest and most perennially enticing of these is "the lane," a wide path carpeted with pine needles that ascends a slope into what appears to be the depths of an enchanted forest. Actually the trail ends abruptly at a screen of woods that conceals development on the hill beyond, in what were once the fields and orchards of the farm before they were sold off. The road was the old farm lane by which hay, grain, and apples were brought down the hill the homestead below. The enchanted forest is hardly primeval. McLaughlin planted all the trees, some now forty or fifty years old, in the open fields that surrounded

the house when he came. His original purpose was to conserve moisture. "The soil was very sandy, and I decided if I was going to have a garden, I would have to have soil conservation. It's proved very effective." The native hardwoods and conifers look as though they have been there forever.

The lane is at its fullest glory in spring, when hundreds of indigenous and exotic wildflowers and their domesticated cousins awake to the young sun's rays filtering through budding trees. Hepaticas are the first to bloom, in early April. They are soon joined by a procession that burgeons in May and June, then continues more modestly right up through September's late asters, gentians, and the colorful berries of some of the spring bloomers.

"I'm very proud of my hepaticas," says McLaughlin as he points out the locations of various members of his large collection. "This

The Grand Masters of Maine Gardening

one is from Japan, a blue one. It's different from ours. The blossom is double. But it isn't any prettier than our native hepaticas." Other hepaticas have crossbred repeatedly until he now has eight to ten different colors. He notes a Tibetan poppy someone has given him and pauses to discourse on epimedium (barrenwort), calling it very adaptable to the wild garden because of its hardiness and early blooming date. Its usual colors are rose, lilac, yellow, or white, but sometimes, he says, "you get a beautiful marking that isn't typical, if your shade and soil are right—a bronzy red—and the foliage goes along with the flower."

He describes a white trillium with characteristic enthusiasm: "Oh, it's a beautiful thing! People just go wild over it. I started with one, and the birds carried the seed over into the field, and now there are hundreds. It naturalizes very easily." McLaughlin's unflagging interest has resulted in extensive collections of lady's slippers, primulas, and dozens of other wild and woodland species. In particular he is noted for his irises and lilacs (he is a member of the American Iris Society, the Maine Iris Society, having served the latter several times as president, and the National Lilac Society), but ferns clearly occupy a privileged place in McLaughlin's heart. "That fern came from China. A lady gave it to me," he explains as he strolls amid the verdure. "And that crested fern is from Oregon. This is a Goldie fern and here's the great fern and the rattlesnake fern. You know," he confides with his little smile, "I always tell people when they're planting ferns to be sure to plant them close to a rock and they'll never lose them. Your rock keeps the soil cool and retains the moisture." Japanese silver (painted) ferns, notable for their delicately marked leaves and russet stems, abound. "See that one beside the rock? See how much better it does?" he points out.

"You know, I'm a foliage man," McLaughlin continues. "Foliage is always satisfying. I had two ladies come from Massachusetts two years ago. 'It's kind of late,' I told them. 'You won't see much in bloom.' 'But this is beautiful!' they said. They were real gardeners. A lot of people, if they don't get a big lot of color, think it isn't much. But it's the foliage and the different greens that make it interesting, and the light and shadows."

McLaughlin's fascination with hens and chickens, those little succulent rosettes found in every rock garden, is a case in point. Anyone who has ever dismissed hens and chickens as dull would reconsider upon seeing the surprising array he has assembled. "I wanted you to see this rock," he says. "Isn't that something?" Indeed it is. Like a colony of spiky sea urchins and anemones on a coral reef, hens and chickens of amazing diversity bask in the rippling shade of beeches and maples. The rock itself is a bizarre natural sculpture of miniature crags and cave-like planting pockets.

> *"I'm a foliage man. Foliage is always satisfying."*

"We moved these rocks in with a double team and drag, hauling that big one very gingerly so's not to bruise it. That must have been forty years ago. I thought I'd make it a cornerstone of my garden. And it's worked out well." Over the years McLaughlin gradually replaced ordinary hens and chickens with more distinctive specimens in an extraordinary range of colors and shapes—pinks, graygreens, a little white "cobweb" type.

"I do have some nice ones," McLaughlin admits. "They're very adaptable and they're very lovely. If I had enough suitable rocks, I'd like to work with hens and chickens and nothing else. They grow well in light shade. See how the moss comes in, and the lichens. They all blend together. You put a few on a rock with a little dirt, press them down, and that's it!"

Nearby, on McLaughlin's deceptively inconspicuous front lawn, are some of the most interesting in his collection of trees. A cedar was raised from seed brought back to him from the gates of a palace in China. A colorful deciduous group includes a dark-leaved Norway maple, a striking Rivers (copper) beech, and what McLaughlin calls the highlight of his garden, a tricolor beech. "So many people from away have never seen one," he's quick to point out. "They're quite rare in Maine. They will thrive here if you have the patience to wait. This is about thirty years old. I think I got it from Wayside Gardens. It's a bit drab now, because it's been dry all summer. But boy, in the spring...!"

McLaughlin's appreciation for the subtle variations of tone and texture that can be found within a single species is nowhere more evident than in his hosta collection. But he's a practical man as well. "I couldn't grow grass there," he says, indicating a shaded northeast corner at the juncture of house and barn, "so I planted hostas." Only a few individuals look familiar in the spectrum of foliage from deep green to white, and the spread in size from miniature to giant.

For all its serenity, Bernard McLaughlin's garden is hardly austere. A shifting pattern of color follows the unfolding season. In May, long ranks of daffodils define the eastern boundary. "I like them by themselves," says McLaughlin. "You can landscape with them if you design your garden that way, but I don't like a bunch here and a bunch there." Other spring bulbs have their own space, too, rather than among the perennials.

At the edge of the sunny meadow lie the broad beds that produce many elegant specimens for the annual Maine Iris Society show in June. Like his daffodils, the tall bearded irises have their own place of honor, but Siberians can be found throughout the garden. Among them is a green-throated white one named 'Bernard McLaughlin' by Currier McEwen. Not surprisingly, in his fifty years of avid gardening McLaughlin has influenced generations of Maine gardeners. Joan and Russell Moors, whose magnificent collection of irises in Auburn includes five hundred varieties, credit him with getting them started.

Masses of brilliant azaleas and rhododendrons adorn the wooded paths in spring, and flowering shrubs of dazzling diversity occupy choice locations. Most of McLaughlin's famous lilacs, numbering about a hundred varieties, are concentrated in a major display area. Unable to single out a favorite, he says there are about ten he would consider tops. Among them he lists 'Mirabelle', an unusual violet color and "a beautiful performing lilac." 'Ludwig Spaeth' he likes for its red-purple bloom. "'Vestale' is as nice a white as you can get, a pure white, a good grower. 'Madame Anton Bruckner' is a very stylish pink."

Daylilies provide important color all summer because they grow well in partial shade, McLaughlin says. "If you'll notice, I have a lot of shade. Anytime you come here there's always bloom somewhere. People ask how I get things to bloom in the shade. Well, the soil is very sandy. Perhaps the plants wouldn't do so well if the soil was heavy."

Phlox and true lilies are his major mid- to late-summer bloomers. McLaughlin laughs as he points out a very ordinary looking magenta phlox. "That's a named variety. Would you believe it?" Along with many elegant modern hybrids, he cherishes a number of old-fashioned ones. "That white one with the pink center is 'Bridesmaid'," he comments, "from an old garden across the street. I've always liked it." At the center of the garden, lilies gleam here and there amid otherwise unremarkable end-of-summer foliage. McLaughlin singles out a striking specimen. "That's 'Jamboree Red'. It's seven feet tall." He stakes all his lilies, but otherwise their requirements are simple, he says: "Good soil and fertilizer in the spring, and that's about it."

Indeed, "good plants, good soil, good care" is McLauglin's complete gardening philosophy. He claims to have no tricks or secrets. It all comes to him quite naturally, he suggests, part of growing up on a farm in Limestone. "We grew potatoes. I always had a vegetable garden. I started a flower garden up home . . . and this is the result," he says wryly, well aware of the quantum leap his statement implies.

During the lengthy interim, he was a self-styled "hack-of-all-trades." He continued to work on the family farm until he was thirty-five, spending his winters as a chef in Florida hotels, which may account for the incongruous hint of southern drawl that colors his northern Maine accent. He came to South Paris in 1936 when he married Rena Tribou, a former class-mate at a Portland business school. She had inherited the old farm, originally purchased as a retirement home by her father, a Bucksport sea captain. For three years McLaughlin com-muted by bus to work in a Portland shipyard and later worked some twenty years in a select grocery store in Norway.

Nineteen years ago he retired to become a full-time gardener. "I'm still getting it orga-nized," McLaughlin quips. He told his wife he was going to have a garden with unusual plants from everywhere so when they got too old to travel, they would have something to enjoy.

DEAN ABRAMSON

True lilies do not require special care, but it is wise to stake them. This is the very popular 'Stargazer'.

Rena, of whom he speaks with deep affection, died three years ago. "She was a wonderful person," he says, "and we had a wonderful life. . . . I miss her awfully, but you have to look at those things in a sensible light. The garden is a great satisfaction. She never worked in the garden, but she enjoyed it to the fullest."

South Paris has changed drastically in the fifty years McLaughlin has lived there. Most of the old houses along Main Street have been torn down. He doesn't mind the noisy high-way going by his door "because I don't stay out front." The master gardener has also no-ticed changes in overall attitudes toward lawns and gardens. "I don't know whether I set a precedent or not, but my lawns have always

The varied textures and subtle colors of hens and chickens beautifully offset native fieldstones and their lichens. Hens and chickens can thrive in light shade as well as sun.

looked impeccable—except this summer. I've never had a lawn such a sight! But as you drive through the outskirts of town now, you see how lawns are kept up and people have planted a lot of trees."

As far as his methods are concerned, McLaughlin gardens "the same as always, because it came naturally to me." His lawn-care formula is fertilizer (5-10-5, which he uses for almost everything) and seeding where necessary. He composts all his leaves and uses chemical fertilizer because manure is almost impossible to get locally—certainly a major change in what was once a farming community. Bags of fertilizer and Pro-Mix potting soil crowd the old stalls in the barn. He uses a dozen bales of the latter each summer to improve the soil as he rebuilds garden beds, and has a truckload of topsoil hauled in every spring as well. Just inside the barn door, a step from the garden, is an old school chair with a writing arm, at which he prepares the labels that mark virtually everything in the garden. Here also he makes an immediate record of every plant he puts in "so I won't forget to do it later." More formal records are kept at leisure in the house.

It's easy to grow things here, he says of the South Paris area. "If we have a good snow cover in the winter to protect the plants, you can grow almost anything. I have no problems with anything I try to grow. I just don't order anything that's semi-hardy."

At eighty-eight, McLaughlin doesn't feel particularly limited by his age, though he gets up from a kneeling position rather carefully. "Perhaps I have cut down a bit," he admits. And he's begun to ask people to stop giving him more plants. He hasn't run out of interest or energy but he's run out of room.

McLaughlin continues to follow a regimen of constant cultivation. "I don't have many weeds, but unless the soil is really humusy, you have to loosen it up. Those hepaticas— I've gone through them twice this summer." All of this he does himself. His only assistant is his cousin, Cyril McLaughlin, who comes down from East Millinocket to spend summers with him. Cyril mows lawns, hooks up hoses, spreads loam, and does other heavy chores. Except for a woman who comes in to clean once a week, McLaughlin looks out for himself in winter, and makes plans for spring.

The secret of a long, healthy life, says McLaughlin, is found in the garden. "Sharing it with others is my great satisfaction. I think perhaps the greatest pleasure is watching things grow. It's so beautiful in the spring, watching those ferns coming up gradually, day by day. And of course, the bloom you get all summer long. I intend to keep on gardening as long as God permits."

Roger Luce,
Maine's Dean of Magnolias

Roger Luce, who died on November 29, 2002, at the age of eighty-two, was the last of the three "grand masters of Maine gardening" I had the privilege of meeting, while Currier McEwen was the first. All the other gardeners I've written about I met during the twenty years between these memorable visits.

Delicate spring green was just beginning to dust the apple trees in the old orchard and the branches of the hardwoods among the dark conifers on the surrounding hillside. Roger Luce, the last resident of the Newburgh homestead that has been in his family since the early 1800s, moved with an octogenarian's thoughtful pace along the grassy, daffodil-bordered path. He stopped, that cool May morning, before many a small tree with white or pink or rosy bloom bursting from its leafless limbs, to explain the attributes and ancestry of these beauties that have earned him the honorific "Dean of Maine Magnolias."

Maine magnolias? The very thought astonishes the average gardener familiar with the limitations imposed by our hard winters and reluctant springs. But not Roger Luce. He grew them, created many new ones, and sold them to knowing gardeners in Maine and beyond for more than fifty years. I had the good fortune to visit him in the year before he died.

Luce made growing magnolias in Maine sound easy. "They're very healthy. They don't need much care," he told me, conceding that establishing them could be a little difficult. "It takes two or three years to get them rooted in, but there's no special way of planting. Like anything else, you just dig a hole and put it in.

Just regular garden soil, well drained. Magnolias can't stand water at their roots." Neither do they appreciate drought, which has been a problem in recent summers.

Moderate moisture, Maine's acid soils, and a boost with 10-10-10 fertilizer as needed keep magnolias happy, and they need little pruning. They flower from late April to the end of June as different varieties come into bloom. Late frost can nip the flowers, but the plants are perfectly hardy. Buds for the next year's blossoms, "like little pussy willows," Luce described them, form during the summer. Depending on the variety, magnolias reach from three to more than fifty feet in height and bloom at anywhere from three to fifteen years of age.

Although the classic Southern magnolias, with their broad petals and shiny leaves, can be grown in Maine, Luce always worked with the types native to north-temperate climates, pushing the limits of the more delicate ones. "The *stellata* [star] magnolias are all hardy," he said. "They're the earliest to bloom. This one bloomed April 27, the first to open." 'Spring Snow', 'Waterlily', 'Ballerina', 'Orchid', 'King Rose' (from New Zealand) are among the well-known *stellata* hybrids, which have varying numbers of open, lacy petals, as their name suggests. The *soulangiana*s are a little tricky to grow, Luce said. "Sometimes the flower buds might winterkill, but the plant lives." The *denudata*s are more tender. Originally they, and their fellow *liliiflora* magnolias, were introduced in the West by Sir Joseph Banks, who collected them in China in 1798 when he was the botanist on Captain Cook's trip around the world. "The *denudata*s are very fragrant," Luce continued, "and the *stellata* hybrids are, too. Here's a cross between a *stellata* and a *kobus*, one of my best seedlings. The frost got the flowers because it blooms so early.

"That one is 'Spring Snow'. It's very fragrant. This is 'Waterlily'. It's a little pinkish. The big one in back is 'Merrill'. Some people call it 'Dr. Merrill', but that's not correct," said the humbly erudite horticulturist. "I got that from the Arnold Arboretum [in Jamaica Plain, Massachusetts] in 1950. It's done well." The small man with a full head of soft gray hair and a kindly, quiet manner pointed with his cane toward another handsome shrub. "I got the seed for the white one over there from plants in front of the Beijing Hotel in 1983. That it has lived here is a miracle." Luce was a member of the first botanical excursion to China and Korea, one of three trips he made to the Far East in 1979, 1981, and 1983. He took gifts of seeds and books to his hosts. The seeds and plant materials he received in return have become an important part of his garden.

Magnolias were blooming everywhere among the old apple trees, rhododendrons, azaleas, hydrangeas, dogwoods, tree peonies, and the intruding brush that Luce was no longer able to keep at bay. But he knew where to look for them. "I was fortunate to have the first bloom in Maine of one of the loveliest, the new yellow 'Elizabeth'," he told me. "Down there I have some tree magnolias, *kobus borealis*, from Japan. They're very hardy. In some places, they get up to fifty feet."

"Down there" were the fields of daylilies he grew in vast numbers and a pond surrounded by azaleas and more magnolias. His gardens also included outstanding specimens of crab apples, lilacs, and any number of perennials.

Luce spent much of his life propagating magnolias and other shrubs and plants once thought to be too delicate to grow in Maine. "He had the attitude that fir trees are not the only thing that grows in Maine," says Rick Sawyer of Fernwood Nursery, one of Luce's close friends and collaborators in plant propagation. "He grew a London plane tree once, just because he liked them. He finally lost it, but it was two feet high before it died." Sawyer calls Luce one of the forefathers of horticulture in Maine, along with Bernard McLaughlin, memorialized in the McLaughlin Gardens in South Paris; Currier McEwen, interna-tionally known hybridizer (still seeking the ultimate Japanese iris at age 102); and the late Lyle Littlefield, who

KEVIN SHIELDS

Roger Luce spent a lifetime demonstrating that magnolias can indeed thrive in Maine.

established the horticulture program at the University of Maine. "They were people who went after horticulture with a zeal and a love long before gardening became the thing to do," Saywer says. "They just went and tried things people said wouldn't grow here."

Continuing the circuit of the garden on that memorable visit, Luce pointed out a robust rhododendron. "That's one of my seedlings. I haven't [officially] named it yet. It's pinker than the others, so I call it 'Candy Cane'." A fragrant white magnolia nearby was another of his crosses, one of his best, he said. Fifteen years old, it, too, remained unnamed— that is, formally registered and introduced to the market. Luce's extreme shyness was the despair of his friends. He hybridized many plants that should have been introduced to the industry, Sawyer says. "He failed to do so out of modesty. People would look at a plant and say, 'That's a wonderful plant, Roger,' and he'd say, 'Oh well, it's nothing special,' but it really was."

> "Roger Luce had the attitude that fir trees are not the only thing that grows in Maine."

Roger Luce was born and raised on this Penobscot County farm he called Butternut Hill Gardens. He learned to love growing things as he helped his parents with the chores before he went off to college. They kept animals and grew all kinds of old apples. Some of the hundred-year-old trees—William, St. Lawrence, King, Wolf River—still survive. One ancient crab apple dates from 1860. "I keep them now for the shade they provide, mostly for the primroses," he said.

After attending Eastern Maine Normal School in Castine, Luce earned a BS in Education from the University of Maine in 1946 and later an MEd from the University of Connecticut. He also studied at the University of Manchester, England; The American School of Classical Studies in Athens, Greece; and the University of Iran, where he pursued ancient and modern history on a Fulbright Scholarship. In 1955 he was awarded a sabbatical to teach English as a second language at the American School in Giessen, Germany. Wherever he traveled, he made sure to visit gardens. Though he told me that he took only one course in horticulture—as an elective, with Roger Clapp at the University of Maine—he had apparently forgotten those he enrolled in at the New York Botanical Gardens. But his claim that the rest of his horticultural training was "just experience" is indisputable.

For three decades, Roger Luce devoted his life to teaching, for most of that time as a social studies and English teacher and vice principal at Middlesex Junior High School in Darien, Connecticut. But his love of plants continued as he landscaped the school grounds with flowering trees and shrubs and enjoyed his homestead gardens in his time off. Luce retired in 1977 and moved back to the farm to pursue his hobby full-time. He ran a nursery business for a while, but gave it up, more interested in developing his gardens than in commercializing them. His plants continued to get around Maine and beyond, however, as he shared and swapped with friends and acquaintances.

At eighty-two, Luce could only stroll through his plantation to assess and enjoy the fruits of his years of labor—no more brush cutting, pruning, weeding—and, alas, no younger generation to take over the physical work. But Luce's spirit of adventure was keen till the last. He kept it alive making crosses, collecting

Magnolia 'Water Lily'

Roger Luce, Maine's Dean of Magnolias

Magnolia 'Wada's Picture'

seed, and growing seedlings in his greenhouse.

"There's a great variation. You never know what you're going to get," he said with a twinkle, revealing his true Yankee heritage when he added, "Seed is cheaper. You get more plants than you could buy, and if the seedlings are good, they work very well." This was how he stocked his nursery business. "I used to sell a lot of magnolias, lilacs, and some azaleas, three to six feet tall, all from seed. People still come to see me, but I have nothing to sell anymore."

As well as magnolias and rhododendrons, Luce raised cyclamens, peonies, and other perennials in his greenhouse. "There are a lot of different ways to grow from seed. For magnolias, you have to collect the seeds, clean them, and stratify them—put them in plastic bags with peat moss for moisture and put them in cold storage for two months, in the refrigerator, not the freezer." He took a small plastic package from a shelf. "These were stratified for two months, then I brought them in where it's warm and see, they're sprouting. Now I have to transplant them. Magnolias must never dry out. It's an imitation of what happens in nature." Peonies are more complicated, he explained. They have to be kept warm for two months, then cold. "I did even more seed raising when I was able to do all the physical work outside," he said regretfully.

Horticulture was Luce's first love. He belonged to the Magnolia Society, the American Rhododendron Society, the International Lilac Society, the Primula Society, the American Rock Garden Society, the Alpine Garden

The Grand Masters of Maine Gardening

Society, and the Daylily Society. But his interests also included antiques, fine art, ballet, music, photography, serigraphy (silk screening), gourmet cooking, and travel. Though his activities had grown more limited, he never missed his annual pilgrimage to Northeast Harbor to see the spring display of azaleas at the Asticou Gardens or visits to gardens and nurseries around the state.

Although Roger Luce is mentioned in authoritative gardening books and cited by teachers of horticulture around the country, he maintained that his reputation came only from word of mouth. "People have read about me in articles in the *Bangor Daily News*," he reluctantly admitted. He never wrote an article of any kind himself, he insisted. The respect and admiration he won from others was outdone only by his own modesty. When confronted with his achievements, he would claim, "I have no reason to boast."

Hard to believe, considering the many accolades Roger Luce received. Currier McEwen named an iris after him. The Roger Luce Award for "excellence in the use of perennials," given at the annual (Maine) People, Places & Plants Spring Flower and Garden show, was established in 1999. Paul Tukey, of *People, Places & Plants* magazine, explains how it came about: "There was not a man in New England who knew more about plants than Roger. The award came together when I found out that Mark Sellew, who owns Pride's Corner Farm in Connecticut, is a major supplier of plants to garden centers in Maine. Once upon a time, Roger expelled Mark from school for a week for misbehavior and Mark never forgot it. When I asked him to sponsor an award in Roger's honor, he was happy to do it, in honor of a lesson he had learned years ago."

Since Roger Luce's passing, many people have wondered what will become of his garden and its extraordinary collection of plants. Rick Sawyer worked with him for the last few years propagating his plants and recent crosses and making selections from his trial beds. "He wanted me to propagate his plants, and that is an honor," Sawyer says. "Eleanor [Hardy, Luce's sister] and I will see to it that the plants he developed are propagated and named as he wished, and kept safe. When you really think of it, his work will continue anyway by the influence he had on so many people in horticulture. It may not be at a single location or by a single person, but it will continue, simply because he dared to take the first step and encouraged others to do the same." As for the farm itself, the family is enjoying and watching over it. "With every plant that Roger gave to people came the words 'enjoy and share.'" Sawyer recalls. "It was his philosophy and how he dealt with people and plants."

Beatrix Farrand and Betsy Moore,
Master Designer and Disciple

Internationally known garden designer Beatrix Farrand, herself a disciple of the great English landscape architect Gertrude Jekyll, made her summer home at Reef Point in Bar Harbor. Of the gardens she designed for Mount Desert Island residents, only two remain intact—the Abby Aldrich Rockefeller Garden in Seal Harbor and The Farm House Garden in Bar Harbor, which was restored by Betsy Collier (now Moore). The Colliers have divorced since the time of my visit in 1988, but Betsy Moore continues to devote as much time as she can to preserving her reclaimed treasure.

Betsy Collier [Moore] is the curator of a rare horticultural gem, a small garden that could almost be regarded as a national treasure, the last surviving garden in Bar Harbor designed by the legendary Beatrix Farrand. "It's something you have a responsibility to keep going," Betsy says, then adds an important clue to the garden's enduring vitality and fresh charm. "To me it's like part of my soul." Clearly the old-fashioned garden that spills exuberantly onto both sides of a ramrod-straight path leading through first one, then another ancient gate, is as much an expression of Betsy's creative skill and devotion as it is of Beatrix Farrand's genius as a designer.

This garden fills the incomparable "backyard" of The Farm House, a small, sequestered Cape two blocks from downtown Bar Harbor. It's screened from today's motels and housing developments by Farrand's judicious plantings, grown as dense in the last sixty years as the hedge around Sleeping Beauty's castle. Betsy and her husband, Sargent Collier, Jr., inherited the property seven years ago from his great-aunt, Mildred McCormick. The 1810 farmhouse miraculously escaped the devastating forest fires of 1947, thanks, the story goes, to the gardener, who mounted the roof with a hose. Long before the fire, the farm served as a dairy for the now-vanished grand cottages on the hill above, and perhaps as a retreat from their social hubbub for Sargent's great-grandfather McCormick.

The Farm House Garden was designed by Beatrix Farrand in 1928 for her friend and fellow member of the Garden Club of Mount Desert, Miss McCormick. Although Sargent Collier had summered in Bar Harbor since childhood, Betsy discovered the town only after her marriage. A serious gardener who studied landscape design at Radcliffe, she was delighted to learn of Miss McCormick. But she met the lady only briefly, when Miss McCormick was in her nineties. Betsy laments not having had the opportunity to learn more about the garden directly from Aunt Mildred. "It wasn't my house, and we didn't know we were going to inherit it. I couldn't anticipate or find out what I would need to know." The fact that it came to them as a surprise has made the couple treasure the garden even more.

What they found when The Farm House

TOM STEWART

Bright colors predominate in the main garden. Softer, muted tones characterize the first garden "room," beyond the gate in this view. Arborvitae hedges and decorative gates define the three distinct portions of the garden.

Sedums, dusty miller, and sweet woodruff are among the low-growing plants that flank the central footpath.

came into their hands was the skeleton of the Farrand design, its shrubbery overgrown, its beds decked out by successive gardeners in the changing fashions of several decades. Even as early as 1934, it was described in the program for the annual meeting of the Garden Club of America as "a kitchen and flower garden where . . . many-colored annuals are grown in masses of color."

When Betsy encountered it nearly fifty years later, "it looked like an Italian garden stuffed with marigolds," she recalls. "I really had to work to get it back. I knew how we wanted to do it, but it took a while to find out where the old things were and move them back. Now it's a totally authentic Beatrix Far-

rand garden. It's never really been altered, just restored to the original plans."

The word *just* is an understatement of the most flagrant sort. Actually Betsy embarked on a laborious program involving equal parts research, planning, and good, old-fashioned sweat. She began by seeking information from the Beatrix Farrand Archives at the University of California at Berkeley. They were able to furnish copies of the original plans for the main beds in the central garden and detailed drawings of gates, fences, and decorative accessories. The rest Betsy had to discover. She got help from Gary Kohler of the Arnold Arboretum, who advised her on the shrubbery, and Patrick Chassé, who supervises the private Abby Aldrich Rockefeller Garden in Seal Harbor (also designed by Farrand). In addition, she learned a great deal from local people who had worked on the place over the years and remembered the way things used to be. Figuring out a chronology of the plantings from old pictures, which showed the house at different stages of remodeling, she tried to determine just what Farrand had designed and revised herself and what had been added later.

"I really had to study Beatrix Farrand's life and how she did her gardens," Betsy relates. "I studied Gertrude Jekyll, who was her English mentor. I've been to Munstead Wood House, Surrey, to get the flavor of exactly what Jekyll had done. Gertrude had such a great influence on Beatrix. I spent a lot of time at Radcliffe with Eleanor McPeck and Diane McGuire" (authors of *Beatrix Farrand's American Landscapes*). Betsy also did her own "archeological digs," finding remnants of a few plants on their original sites and discovering the benches that Farrand designed hidden in a little playhouse in the back field. Betsy and her gardener-handyman James Day, of Ellsworth, restored them all.

For much of the garden restoration, she had no precise guide. Using the one original plan she had and all the other knowledge she was able to glean, she came up with what she thinks Farrand intended. Looking at an old photograph of the main garden, she observes, "If [you'd trained as a landscape architect], you'd look at the garden and say, 'There's not enough variety here.' The backdrop is wonderful, but there's too much repeated. Maybe somehow it got away from her, or she wanted that real wild look, but she didn't have enough variety in it." Betsy wonders whether Farrand watched the garden mature and revised it from time to time, as all gardeners must. She has taken a certain amount of artistic license in her restoration—"because when you have something like this, especially a famous garden, you want to have variety in it. You want it to have that English flavor, with interesting things in it." For example, Betsy introduced heather, which Farrand hadn't used, to replace some of the pink snapdragons. "The way I've done it now," she continues, "is to use drifts, like Gertrude Jekyll did: a lot of grays on the ends that drift through the colors, then shading from pastels at the house to deeper colors. You don't do it in rows, but sort of triangles, each drift at least six feet wide. It looks like an impressionist painting."

Betsy's restored garden is a statement in its simplest form of the design philosophy that Beatrix Farrand executed elsewhere on a much grander scale. (Among the dozens of private and public gardens that Farrand designed in America and abroad, Dumbarton Oaks, in Washington, D.C., is considered by many to be her finest accomplishment.) Nevertheless,

"I really had to study Beatrix Farrand's life and how she did her gardens."

The Farm House Garden is very much an estate garden. Tall hedges of arborvitae and groupings of shrubs and magnificent trees define spaces—actually outdoor "rooms"—whose calculated proportions promote the illusion of much greater size, a characteristic Farrand ploy.

Betsy explains the choice of a floral wallpaper for Aunt Mildred's little library, from which the central door opens into the garden. "The room is quite dark, and the door is usually open, so you get the feeling of looking into a series of rooms out there." From the door, a pea-stone path follows a straight axis to a white gate in the deep green hedge beyond, its strict line softened by the varied textures in the perennial beds on either side. Whatever pace one chooses for strolling between the sweet-scented alyssum, pansies, pinks, and pungent herbs, one is irresistibly drawn to the white gate with its squirrel ornament, tucked under a dark arch of arborvitae, beckoning like the door to Mary's Secret Garden.

Beyond the gate, the path continues as before, directly to another in the distance, but the visitor is so stunned by the new spectacle that there is no urge to hurry on. In contrast to the quiet, muted colors on the other side of the squirrel gate, this stretch of garden is alive with color: the bright green capelets of lady's mantle juxtaposed along the walk with lacy gray dusty miller, 'Wargrave Pink' geranium, furry gray lamb's ears, and deep blue-purple catmint; the mid-height snapdragons, stocks, and foxgloves in shades of cream and pink; the predictable blue delphiniums towering at the back, set off by brilliant splashes of golden glow, mounds of white phlox, and plumes of lacy lavender meadow rue. It's impossible to move briskly along the path here, so fascinating is the infinite variety of shape and color.

Again, though, the wily Farrand provoked adventure with that second gate at the end of the path, a gate that, as one visitor put it, "must be opened." This time, however, the surprise is of another sort. No more alluring gravel path amid a bower of bloom but instead

One is irresistibly drawn to the white gate with its squirrel ornament.

a very practical Yankee vegetable garden, brightened by flourishes of blazing orange nasturtium. The sixteen-by-sixteen-foot raised-bed complex, surrounded by a stout deer fence and "capable of feeding an army," according to Betsy, is of her own devising. Although no clues remained but some water pipes and a few ancient apple trees, Betsy had heard that Aunt Mildred once had a vegetable garden back here in what was, like the main flower gardens, undoubtedly once a pasture. Beatrix Farrand, who had a prolific vegetable garden at her own Bar Harbor estate (now gone) may even have planned Aunt Mildred's kitchen garden.

About-facing toward the house, now-open gates reveal the astuteness of Farrand's solution for The Farm House Garden. At the far end of the path, beyond the gates and the long swaths of plantings, the diminutive house itself, little more than its low roof and chimneys visible above the hedge, has a distant charm, a touch of romance. Even with the garden's two relatively small "rooms," Farrand achieved the same effect of mystery and surprise that she did at sixteen-acre Dumbarton Oaks.

Returning through the gates into the area next to the house, the contrast to the other garden spaces is noticeable—and Betsy's strategy becomes apparent. "I made this a quiet entry so that when you go through the squirrel gate into the main garden, you get an explosion of color," she explains. "I've got so much color in the main focal point that I made this area a total pink, blue, and white garden with just a hint of yellow—a soft, quiet garden." Here, too, is the little terrace that Farrand added, perfect for a summer breakfast or evening cocktails.

Betsy has put considerable effort into restoring the one-and-a-half-story farmhouse itself, not with major remodeling but with meticulous attention to detail. "Just sprucing it up makes it seem younger, but keeping the flavor of the old" is how she describes it. A little workroom off the kitchen is Betsy's gardening nerve center. Here she keeps her books, plant lists, and a large-scale master garden plan. It's pinned up and revised every spring and subject to further changes as inspiration dictates. Copies go into the garden, where she and her helper, James Day, work from them.

She admits that maintaining the garden is a lot of work, but she has been able to find excellent assistance. The maintenance routine includes taking up and dividing all perennials every second year, "to keep on top of it," cutting back old stalks every October, and mulching with pine boughs and straw. "We always do whatever the Rockefeller gardens are doing," Betsy confesses cheerfully. "If they're getting sewage-treatment sludge, the same people deliver it to us."

The Collier children—Leandra, thirteen, Eliza, eight, and Sargie, six—feel pretty much as their mother does about the garden. "They all help," says Betsy. "Getting ready for the open garden day last summer, I was up here just two days before, and I had to do everything because James had been painting the house and doing the heavy trimming. I said, 'Just leave the weeding to me. I can handle that easily.' Well, the kids got right out there and helped. They were terrific. Sargie was sweeping up all the piles of weeds we were throwing down." The children love to play in the gardens, says their mother. "It's like a secret garden to them."

The family's year-round home is a large farm with horses, sheep, llamas, and extensive gardens in Essex, Massachusetts. Though their busy life does not allow them whole summers at The Farm House Garden, the intensity of their experience when they are there is a tacit tribute to Beatrix Farrand's genius and Betsy's interpretation of it.

"It's really wonderful to walk through these gardens, any time of the day or night," she says. "You get a different feeling, a very wonderful, exhilarating feeling. I think everyone has a sense of walking into a special garden that's come out of our grandmothers' era."

Asticou,
A Beatrix Farrand Legacy

As well as in Betsy Moore's Farm House Garden and the Abby Aldrich Rockefeller Garden, Beatrix Farrand's legend lives on elsewhere on Mount Desert Island. Many components of her Reef Point estate are preserved in two settings in Northeast Harbor: the Asticou Azalea Garden and the Thuya Garden (page 40).

    Maintained by the Island Foundation, the Asticou Garden remains pretty much as I saw it in 1989 when I wrote this article. Mary Roper, a graduate of the College of the Atlantic, in Bar Harbor, is the current head gardener for both the Asticou and Thuya Gardens.

Among Mount Desert Island's fabled splendors is one exquisite, small gem so accessible that, ironically, it is often overlooked. Across the road from the elegant old Asticou Inn in Northeast Harbor, at the junction of Routes 3 and 198, lies a garden unlike any other in Maine. Here a small pond, from mid-May to late June, mirrors an astonishing array of colorful blossoms, from palest pinks to ravishing crimsons, set off by the high-flung arches of blossoming crab apple and flowering plum. The Asticou Azalea Garden stops many a casual motorist in springtime and bids him or her wander its pine-carpeted and pink-granite-graveled paths amid a dazzling assortment of azaleas and rhododendrons. Even among regular visitors, few could guess how this horticultural treasure came to be.

In the early twentieth century Beatrix Farrand, one of America's most innovative and successful landscape artists, put her most devoted efforts into gardens at her own Bar Harbor estate, Reef Point, hoping to establish there a permanent institute for horticulture and landscape design research. Several years before her death in 1959, she realized there

was no way to ensure the garden's perpetuation according to her standards, and made plans to have it dismantled. Among the many who mourned the prospective loss was Charles Savage, manager of the Asticou Inn, whose family had lived in the area for several generations. Savage, an amateur landscape designer, undertook to rescue what he could of the Reef Point collection, particularly the azaleas. Farrand's decision to demolish the garden she'd spent a lifetime building was made in 1956. Savage had just a year to find suitable land, design the garden, move the plants, and finance the project. He chose an alder swamp opposite the inn—partly with the pleasure of his guests in mind—had it dredged, and got the pond and major plantings installed by 1957. It was a superhuman task, explains Patrick Chassé, currently the garden's design consultant. "If you go through the garden now, you can see that the watercourse was laid out and lined with dry stone walls," he says, noting that quantities of fill were needed to raise the terraced grounds above the water table to create a suitable environment for planting.

    The result is a small, man-made landscape with all the charm and many of the features of a classic Japanese garden, a style peculiarly suited to Mount Desert's unique ambiance—a cosmopolitan turn-of-the-century elegance set off by the natural drama of pink granite boulders, wind-sculpted pines, and crashing seas. On the Asticou Inn's deck, high above the picturesque little harbor, the mood is almost Mediterranean. Slip back across the road to the azalea garden and the overtones are hauntingly Oriental. Classic stone bridges cross a stream that burbles soothingly into the pond from cool green haunts of fern and jack-in-the-pulpit. Ancient stone lanterns squat mysteriously among the plantings. Benches insist upon lingering contemplation of every artfully proportioned vista.

Charles Savage continued to maintain and refine the Asticou Azalea Garden for nearly twenty years. By the 1970s, however, the inn management began to find the cost of its upkeep prohibitive. The garden was given to the Town of Mount Desert, which in its turn could not afford the horticultural expertise for proper maintenance. Wild blackberries and other native shrubs began their inevitable invasion. Plant labels were lost. Trees that were twenty feet tall when Savage planted them had reached forty feet, losing the original design concept and shading out the understory. "No one knew quite how to make the choice— whether to thin out the trees or let everything under them die," says Chassé.

Fortunately for the future of the Asticou Azalea Garden, a group of summer residents, alarmed by the garden's imminent demise, mustered to form the Island Foundation in 1970 to take over title to the property and begin preservation. An anonymous gift in 1982 made major renovation possible. Patrick Chassé's firm, Landscape Design Associates, of Northeast Harbor, was hired to develop a master plan. Japanese horticulturist Osamu

DAVID RANSAW

Blossoming crab apples and plums provide the backdrop for Asticou's masses of azaleas and rhododendrons.

Shimizu began annual advisory visits. Fred Galle, the country's foremost authority on azaleas and rhododendrons, was called in to begin a five-year identification project. Thomas Hall, vice president of the Island Foundation, became chairman of the garden committee in 1986. "Pat and I were accused of trying to change what Charles Savage did," Hall says, recalling the difficult decision to thin and prune and revamp. "But I think in a way we're . . . trying to preserve what he did by recognizing that it inevitably does change and to retain his spirit by modulating [his design]."

Everywhere the blending of native and exotic, a Farrand methodology that Savage faithfully emulated, creates the fascinating illusion of art following nature, or is it nature following art? Nowhere is this more evident than in the Zen garden, designed for Savage by a Japanese architect. The meticulously raked white sand, with its complement of selected stones, is surrounded by a low wall of patterned tiles and pottery crocks of hens and chickens bordered, surprisingly, by Maine blueberries. Behind it grows a screen of cut-leaf maples and huge cedars. A stone bench overlooks the Zen garden from a nook in the shrubbery, inviting serious meditation.

"Farrand was very interested in finding plants that would naturalize on Mount Desert, be happy here, grow without cultivation," Chassé says. "She imported ericaceous plants [the family that includes azaleas, rhododendrons, and heathers] from all over the world. She also used a lot of native Maine plants at Reef Point. Some of them came here. It's very hard to tell what were hers and what Charles added." Among the Reef Point survivors at Asticou are yews, andromedas, an ancient dwarf Alberta spruce, and an impressive Sargent weeping hemlock, recently pruned to advantage by Shimizu, who bravely wielded shears where no one else had dared. Most

numerous, though, are the azaleas and their relatives.

The Reef Point collection at its height contained more than a thousand specimens, including 250 azaleas, 175 rhododendrons and laurels, and numerous heathers. The Asticou Azalea Garden boasts fifty to sixty varieties of these, Hall estimates, including additions and spontaneous hybrids. Expert Fred Galle was able to identify only about twenty-seven that may have come from Reef Point, says Hall. One stretch of walk along the pond illustrates the immensity of the task. Here are azaleas in every shade of peach, apricot, salmon, melon, shrimp, pink, rose, orange, red, red-orange, scarlet, ad infinitum, to say nothing of differences in size and shape of blossom and leaf or season of bloom. Happily there are as many late as early bloomers, some even waiting until July to open. Some resemble honeysuckle in both form and fragrance, adding a delicious olfactory dimension to the garden's sensory pleasures.

"It's really been the survival of the fittest," says Chassé. "They've made it through the roughest times, which I think makes them more valuable because they're proven survivors in this climate." The Asticou garden, in Mount Desert's sea-tempered miniclimate, is situated in a natural bowl, protected on the northwest by Penobscot Mountain. Azaleas are a cool-climate plant, Chassé points out. In the home garden, they need protection from too much heat as well as severe cold, so the south side of a building could be too hot a location in summer. Hall adds that azaleas should be sheared immediately after blooming to allow buds time to form for the following year.

The Asticou Azalea Garden, because of its easy access and visibility, offers the public the legacy of Beatrix Farrand's constant experimenting, says Chassé. "It's almost a little ar-

DAVID RANSAW

In his garden at Asticou, Charles Savage followed Beatrix Farrand's methodology of blending native and exotic species.

The sound of a small stream and the reflective surface of the pond add to the garden's sensory pleasures.

boretum or study collection. So many people who visit the garden are amazed at how much is there. They say they had no idea something like this would grow here. We're trying to find out what they all are. It's so frustrating when we can't tell people. In many cases, now, with the new material, we can. Visitors can go home and say, 'Gee, I know this might work.' That's educational."

Both educational and beautiful, the

Asticou Azalea Garden is possibly the most colorful salute to springtime in Maine. By midsummer it becomes a quiet study in textures and shades of green, a pleasure of a different sort, but in September it once again blazes forth, this time with all the brilliant hues of a New England autumn. Whatever the season, a visit to the little garden by the side of the road in Northeast Harbor is a memorable experience.

Charles Savage's
Thuya Garden

Another of Charles Savage's tributes to Beatrix Farrand is Northeast Harbor's Thuya Garden, as invisible from casual view as the Asticou Azalea Garden is eye-catching. Here Savage preserved plant material from Farrand's Reef Point estate and her artistic vision. Here, also, Savage seamlessly incorporated the wild and the cultivated. Thuya Garden, now under the umbrella of the Island Foundation, continues to evolve. Concern over heavy foot traffic has led to a few modifications since this article first appeared, in 1994. Admission is still free, but contributions left in the donation box are greatly appreciated. Mary Roper is the current head gardener.

When Reef Point was dismantled, Farrand moved to her final residence, a specially designed annex at Garland Farm in Salisbury Cove that incorporated many architectural elements and horticultural treasures from Reef Point. At this writing, a campaign was under way to preserve Garland Farm and perhaps someday realize Farrand's dream of a horticultural research center.

One of the pleasantest short hikes on Mount Desert Island isn't in fabled Acadia National Park, but its surprise ending is as rewarding in its own way as the view from the top of Cadillac Mountain. Next time you're meandering along Route 3 out of Northeast Harbor, stop at the parking area marked "Asticou Terraces" and prepare for a treat. Climb the rock-hewn steps across the way and take the trail that winds steadily upward through the spruce and cedar forest, emerging at comfortable intervals for ever more exalted views of the harbor below and the Cranberry Isles offshore. Sheltered seats at these overlooks, the Asticou Terraces, invite you to stop, to breathe, to behold, perhaps to meditate.

Resume the needle-strewn path and thread your way along fern-hung walls of rosy island granite and among mossy tree trunks that rise from the shadows like columns in some primeval cathedral. Suddenly you find yourself in a clearing as magical as any in the Black Forest. There's an enchanted cottage and a cedar stockade fence whose thick wooden gates are carved with an eclectic iconography: a lamb from a 1629 gardening book, Native American symbols, owls and deer and squirrels, fiddleheads and lady's slippers and jack-in-the-pulpits. Through the open gates, you glimpse green lawns and elegantly laid out flower beds flashing their brilliant colors.

No, you're not in a fairy tale. You have arrived at Thuya Lodge and Thuya Garden. With a history as fascinating as its geography, the park includes the lodge, garden, terraces, and some two hundred acres of neighboring woods and mountainside.

Thuya Lodge, a typical, though unusually modest, example of a turn-of-the-century Mount Desert "rustic" cottage, was the summer home of Joseph Henry Curtis, a Boston

At Thuya, a formal garden emerges gracefully from the rocky, wooded natural backdrop.

landscape architect. It now houses a remarkable botanical library. The name comes from
the abundance of American white cedar, *Thuja
occidentalis*, in the area. (Thuya is an older
spelling.) Curiously, it was not Curtis who designed the garden just a stone's throw from his
cottage. In fact, he never even saw this garden.
His creation was the terraces, named for this
Asticou section of Northeast Harbor. Curtis
died in 1928, leaving his entire property in
trust to the town of Mount Desert "for the
recreation and enjoyment of its residents and
their guests." It was Charles K. Savage, a lifelong resident of the area, the first adminis-

trator of the Asticou Terraces Trust and himself a gifted landscape designer, who conceived
the garden some twenty-five years later.

Inspired by the idyllic setting and the
ready availability of some extraordinary plants
from Beatrix Farrand's Reef Point estate,
Savage cleared the overgrown orchard,
smoothed up the mountainside's rugged contours, and laid out a formal garden on a north-
south axis. Here is a more direct reference to a
cathedral than just the suggestive power of the
woods. Perennial borders as richly colored as
stained glass windows define the nave and
transept and their crossing near the southern

In the bed bordering the long main aisle, pink astilbe adds soft color where the spectrum shifts gradually from bright, warm tones to cool blues and silvers.

the grassy aisle rises between the flower borders in two terraced levels and ends in a simple wooden pavilion among rhododendrons, yews and junipers, ferns, and bunchberries that blend gently into the surrounding woods.

"One of the manifestations of Savage's genius was his ability to make the formal statement against the informality of the landscape," explained Denholm M. Jacobs, the current trustee of the park, and one of my guides when I visited Thuya, along with Timothy Taylor, the property's superintendent. "There's a contrapuntal effect that I think is part of the magic of the garden," Jacobs said. "Here you have the most beautiful natural landscape, put here by God. Savage took advantage of the placement of the stones and the trees and put in these herbaceous borders, for which the background is perfect."

Thuya Garden today is essentially the same garden that Charles Savage designed and developed forty years ago, though some recent visitors might disagree. Savage was a friend and disciple of the great American landscape designer Beatrix Farrand, who summered in Bar Harbor. She designed the famous Rockefeller garden in Seal Harbor, among others on the island and around the world. As well as Mrs. Farrand's artistic vision, Savage put into Thuya Garden a great deal of her actual plant materials, moved from her Bar Harbor estate in 1953. Azaleas, rhododendrons, mountain laurel, some of the long-lived perennial flowers, and the Alberta spruces that act as gateposts to major paths came from Reef Point. Decorative elements such as a handsome 1758 lead water tank and stone urns by Gouldsboro potter Eric Soderholtz were also Mrs. Farrand's.

But trees grow taller and thicker, flower beds become jungles, and winters take their

end. Below this, stone steps lead down to a shallow reflecting pool. The tall "canoe" cedar that stands guard over the pool, and the raked gravel beneath its crystal waters, lend an Oriental touch to this part of the garden. A wooded path leads to a half-hidden, pagodalike summerhouse. In the opposite direction,

The Grand Masters of Maine Gardening

toll. By the late l980s Thuya Garden wasn't looking its best. Jacobs asked Patrick Chassé, of the Northeast Harbor firm of Landscape Design Associates, for a diagnosis. "My first impression was that it was overgrown. Plants needed more light and air. Proportions I remembered seeing as a child were way off-balance," Chassé says. "What really needed to be done was to restore the borders." He did some research, found old photographs, and discovered that, "sure enough, it was a different beast from when it was first created."

Although the old pictures confirmed what Chassé suspected, he could find no detailed drawings of the original garden, only a conceptual plan. Knowing of Savage's intent to preserve the collections and spirit of Reef Point, he decided to come up with a planting plan based on Farrand's concepts. "We tried to use what was still there that I was sure had really come from Reef Point, like the *Echinops* [globe thistle] and *Helianthus*. Those had gotten to be gargantuan masses. We used a fraction of them, so there's a continuous line to some of the [original] materials."

Chassé also added a lot of old favorites and included new varieties, recognizing that both Savage and Farrand would always have been experimenting. "One thing Mr. Savage did so skillfully, and I take great inspiration from his work," Chassé says, "was to achieve a double-sided English border, one of the hardest things to do. It's much easier to back it up against a hedge or a fence. He made something you could walk around, in the middle of this beautiful setting of native plants, mosses, blueberries, ferns.

"When I first saw Thuya Garden in 1986, there was no correlation between the plantings and the woodland setting. Standing between the two borders, I couldn't see over the ranks of seven-foot delphiniums and dahlias or discern any pattern or shape in the blaze of color. Now the borders present a pleasing balance of varied heights, textures, and hues."

There was a certain amount of controversy over the restoration, Chassé says. A lot of people who had seen the garden only in recent years thought that was the way it was supposed to be. "But everyone has come around," he notes. "It's attracted a lot of support, and the trust has gone on to make other improvements, repairing the lodge and the fences." (Boldly decorative as the fences are, their primary purpose is to keep out the deer.)

Even an untutored garden lover can appreciate the subtle sequence of color in Thuya's luxuriant flower beds. Chassé has retained the warm center of Savage's plan. At the crossing, the only bit of the garden that can be seen from the lodge, a sunny tapestry catches the eye. Yellow marigolds, golden sundrops, orange calendulas, pale yellow snapdragons, and light orange 'Stella d'Oro' daylilies are highlighted by low white ageratum, tall, creamy Queen-of-the-Prairie (*Filipendula rubra*) and a few pinks and lavenders.

As you look uphill toward the shady pavilion at the end of the long aisle, the color spectrum cools gradually, from paler yellows to whites and pinks—astilbes, phlox, zinnias, daylilies—then on into lavenders and purples—pansies, *Thalictrum*, monkshood—and finally into the great range of wonderful blues, whites, and silvers—every shade of delphinium, steely globe thistle, heliotrope, catmint, veronica, 'Silver Mound' artemisia. The taller plants are judiciously spaced and

> *"One thing Mr. Savage did so skillfully . . . was to achieve a double-sided English border."*

lacy, offering a variety of pattern and texture in a light, open atmosphere within the embrace of the dark evergreen forest. The effect is one of inspired charm.

There's a science to this charm, Chassé points out. "When you look up the long axis, the foreground is warm. As it goes down the spectrum into cooler colors at the end, it stretches the perspective, because warm colors come towards you and cool colors recede. The border looks longer uphill. When you look downhill it's compressed. It's a little optical trick."

With his astute mingling of art and nature, Charles Savage had created a fascinating tension between the formal and the random. He covered a rock outcropping near the pond with a curving bank of heather and succulents. He preserved one of the old apple trees in Joseph Curtis's orchard as a foil for the horizontal line of the west border. Timothy Taylor couldn't say for sure what variety it is, but "You get a pie out of that tree, you're going have another one," he asserts dryly.

Taylor says he has no special tricks for producing the garden's lush greenery and brilliant color. "Basically, manure when we can, 5-10-5, what have you. We take a soil test every three to six months and redo the beds when they need it," he says. He attributes the good, strong color of the delphiniums to the location, near enough to the sea for high humidity, far enough away to avoid salt spray. Jacobs adds that preventive maintenance by a full-time gardening crew catches problems as soon as they arise.

The crew also takes care of two hundred acres of grounds, maintaining the woodlands, the trails up the mountainside, and the dock on the harbor below—a good place to start for sailors who need to stretch their sea legs.

From Thuya Garden you can hike up Eliot Mountain or over to the Jordan Pond House for popovers and tea. "We all share the responsibility," Jacobs says, "but this modest fellow here [Taylor] is in charge of handling it all. I have a title, but he does the hard work."

No one enjoys Thuya Garden more than these men who work hand in hand. "When I come back in the evenings, I'll just meditate," Taylor says. "I've been working here for nineteen years in September, and I love every bit of it."

"The joy of this place is its tranquility, its size, its simplicity," Jacobs says. "Being able to sit here quietly and reflect upon what one is seeing, read a book, ruminate, is part of the magic of it."

This creates a serious dilemma for both men. In fact, it was with grave reservations that Jacobs allowed *Down East* to tell Thuya's story. The garden is open to the public, and although the terms of Curtis's trust had in mind the local community and their guests, there's no practical way to limit admission to area residents. The garden is small and, like any natural setting, ultimately fragile. "We love to have people enjoy it, treasure it. On the other hand, we fear going past the threshold of capacity," Jacobs says. "If the lawns get trampled, they can't breathe. Too much noise cancels the purpose of meditation."

You can drive up to Thuya if you must. The road is narrow, winding, and bumpy, inaccessible to tour buses, which are not allowed in any case. The parking lot at the garden accommodates no more than a dozen cars. A leisurely, contemplative walk up the Terraces from the Route 3 parking lot is by far the best route to Thuya Garden, where your quiet demeanor and respect will be repaid a thousand-fold by its serene beauty.

Patrick Chassé
Designs a Garden for Mainers

Patrick Chassé's dedication to the Beatrix Farrand legacy continues, though he is no longer the official consultant for Asticou and Thuya Gardens. He is currently writing, lecturing, and designing major landscape projects from Maine to Europe. His most recent is an Ottoman villa on the Bosporus, in Istanbul, Turkey—"a fascinating opportunity for cross-cultural comparison," he says. True to his Aroostook County roots, however, he maintains his spiritual base in Maine, returning frequently to design gardens in his beloved native state. Eleven years ago, Down East *asked him to suggest a plan for an ideal Maine garden.*

I think of the garden as a stage, where the spotlight moves to different characters in a play," says Patrick Chassé, one of Maine's foremost landscape designers. "As things bloom, they are spotlighted, while others recede because they're just foliage." This is just one of the "secrets" that lend Chassé's gardens a singular enchantment—and keep him hopping from client to client, from sumptuous estate gardens on Mount Desert to stylishly landscaped yards in Camden and suburban Portland.

Like most veteran Maine gardeners, Chassé knows from trial and error just what works and what doesn't. He's always learning and, characteristically, always sharing what he's discovered. In fact, when asked to design the "ideal Maine garden"—a thought provoking, if somewhat preposterous question—he took the request seriously. From the list of more than six hundred plants he's worked with that are suitable for the not always hospitable growing conditions down east, he selected a mere thirty-seven that are hardy, colorful, harmonious, and virtually fail-safe for gardeners of every stripe. The result is, in his words, "a

modest border for a regular Maine yard, one that will work against a backdrop of a building, fence, or shrub hedge." It would complement a two-hundred-year-old Cape as well as a brand-new postmodern architectural statement. And it's a border where the show lasts dependably from May to October, reaching a colorful climax in July and August.

"I don't have any idea what the context might be," Chassé is quick to point out, "so what I'm trying to provide is a panel that has color, texture, and sculptural quality and a contemporary aspect, all in balance, without anything that stands out too strongly. There's supposed to be something blooming at all times, some tall, some shorter, some spiky, some rounded—a kind of tweed of time and color and texture."

Chassé calls this calculated succession of bloom "stretching the orchestration of timing." How's that? "When you see a flower garden where absolutely every plant is in bloom all at once," he explains, "it's too rich. It's very contrived. It's human conceit to try to control things that much. It's what I call an unnatural act." His ideal garden has a free-

The showy, though short-lived, scarlet blossoms of Oriental poppies are traditional favorites in Maine gardens.

NANCE TRUEWORTHY

bor firm of Landscape Design Associates; Boston, where he teaches landscape design, landscape history, and plant ecology at Radcliffe and the Arnold Arboretum; and New York City, where he's participating in the renovation of the New York Botanical Garden. He has also lectured in England and is a frequent visitor to Japan, where he's researching that country's venerable garden history for a future teaching assignment.

It's hardly surprising, then, that his ideal Maine border is as practical as it is artistic, as down-home traditional as it is sophisticated. That's why the hollyhocks he chooses, for instance, are the single pink or white old-fashioned ones, not the frilly double ones that "look like carnations." The lupines he recommends are not the elegant, multicolored Russell hybrids but the deep blue ones you could dig up in any meadow in Maine.

"I call this a Maine garden," says the soft-spoken, smooth-faced Maine native who, as the situation demands, can be comfortably down-to-earth or formally academic, "because it's meant to reflect the growing season. You get things that are symbolic of spring, of summer, of autumn. You get a sense of that time and season—very much an aspect of life here."

Beginning with the columbines and irises in May, there's a pattern of color and texture throughout the season, strongest in July and August, tapering into autumn with sedum and asters, and always with a diverse mixture of the foliage and plants yet to blossom or long past it. Peony leaves turned golden and the tawny sheaves of bloomed-out irises are as much a part of the fall color scheme as the asters' rich purples.

"What makes a border look full and wonderful is to plan it so that both the early

form quality to blossoming, not unlike the meadows and roadside fields across the state.

Chassé comes by his expertise in Maine gardening naturally: He grew up in Aroostook County. At forty-four, he divides his time these days between Mount Desert Island, where he is a principal in the Northeas Har-

The Grand Masters of Maine Gardening

bloomers, which have to be cut back, and those that won't bloom till much later have something in front of them that grows at a complementary rate so it hides the hole," Chassé explains. "It has to give the illusion, like a stage set, that it's all filled when in fact there are pockets ebbing and flowing at different times."

Chassé's design calls for a garden that is eight by twenty-five feet, the absolute minimum dimensions that he feels allow for a critical mass of bloom with that necessary feeling of ebb and flow. "The most common mistake," he says, "is to make a garden that's too skimpy in depth. Three to four feet is not enough depth to have a low, medium, and high range of plants. They all get pushed down to an area only a foot or eighteen inches deep and start to look like strips. You don't have enough space to really weave things together." Perennials need a lot of space, up to three feet for a single plant of some of the larger species. In fact, even one plant of some species, such as the popular Shasta daisy, would be too sprawling for the scale of this particular garden, Chassé says.

Color is a matter of personal taste, Chassé's being for the softer shades of pink, blue, lavender, yellows, and white that blend harmoniously. "I stay away from anything too hot," he says, "although if people like hotter pinks, the whole thing can be shaded more to hotter colors. I'm very leery of orange, which is really difficult to blend. The [scarlet-orange] Oriental poppies are very strong but short-lived, one of the highlights that's quickly past, a sort of brief crescendo in the season. The tiger lily [which blooms much later] is orange, too, but its texture is very rich among a lot of blues and greens." The daylilies in the plan aren't the old-fashioned tawny orange ones,

but 'Catherine Woodbury', a creamy yellow with a lavender blush.

Chassé suggests the traditional deep purple Siberian irises. "The only modern hybrid I might use," he says, "is a repeater, one that continues to bloom." As for the tall bearded iris, he recommends "anything but the ones that look like orchids. I see a yellow, with white falls, or a clear blue and yellow." Again, old-fashioned types.

Another vital aspect of balance in this garden is in terms of the amount of work required. That's why this is a perennial garden, composed mainly of faithful bloomers that come up every year from established roots, bulbs, and tubers. Chassé includes a mere handful of dependable annuals, such as alyssum, snapdragons, and calendulas (pot marigolds), to fill in the odd pocket. If so inclined, one could plant spring bulbs in the small foreground spots and plant over them with annuals when they have gone by, he notes. Although nurseries carry an increasing diversity of perennials, and more avid gardeners even raise them from seed, an important and traditional source, especially for the old-fashioned varieties, is sharing among family, friends, and neighbors, or frequenting local plant sales.

Perennials do need to be divided (as well as weeded), but the ever-practical Chassé points out that the plants he has selected grow at different rates. Some won't need division for a few years, others more often. "It's not 'Oh, God, every other year I have to dig up

> "When you see a flower garden where absolutely every plant is in bloom all at once, it's too rich."

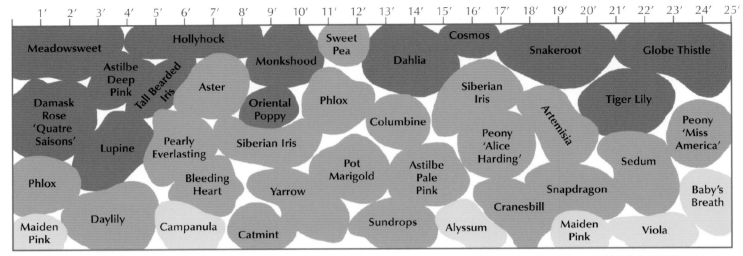

| 1' | 2' | 3' | 4' | 5' | 6' | 7' | 8' | 9' | 10' | 11' | 12' | 13' | 14' | 15' | 16' | 17' | 18' | 19' | 20' | 21' | 22' | 23' | 24' | 25' |

Meadowsweet   Hollyhock   Sweet Pea   Cosmos   Snakeroot   Globe Thistle

Astilbe Deep Pink   Tall Bearded Iris   Monkshood   Dahlia

Damask Rose 'Quatre Saisons'   Aster   Oriental Poppy   Phlox   Siberian Iris   Tiger Lily

Columbine   Artemisia   Peony 'Miss America'

Lupine   Pearly Everlasting   Siberian Iris   Peony 'Alice Harding'   Sedum

Phlox   Bleeding Heart   Pot Marigold   Astilbe Pale Pink   Snapdragon   Baby's Breath

Yarrow   Cranesbill

Maiden Pink   Daylily   Campanula   Catmint   Sundrops   Alyssum   Maiden Pink   Viola

DARK GREEN — TALL (OVER 3')   MEDIUM GREEN — MEDIUM (1'–3')   LIGHT GREEN — SHORT (UNDER 1')

the whole thing and start over!' It's the sort of garden you could allot predictable, short chunks of time to, integrate into your life, not be a slave to it." He also notes that although this is not a cutting garden, containing as it does only one or two of any given species, the extras can be planted in convenient rows in the vegetable garden, where they can be harvested for the house just like the edibles.

The plants Chassé selected for this garden are also what are often called fail-safe or iron-clad, he says—hardy, resistant to pests, and presenting a high pleasure quotient, a high degree of return for the effort. In a way, this explains why Chassé's design omits showy, tall delphiniums regarded by many as so typical of Down East gardens. "Delphiniums are a sort of extravagance," he says. "They give a very limited exposure for the amount of work they involve." Chassé substitutes here the similar tall blue spikes of old-fashioned monkshood,

which, although not quite as spectacular as delphinium, is tougher, rarely requires staking, and has a much longer season of bloom.

The tried-and-true plants in this garden will grow in almost any Maine soil, Chassé says, provided they get sufficient water and nutrients. Organic fertilizers such as cotton-seed meal, blood meal, and bonemeal provide nutrients over a longer period than chemical fertilizers. The incorporation of other organic materials such as compost and composted sewage sludge is very important for soil improvement, he adds.

In sketching out an ideal garden for Mainers, Chassé stresses that his design is not engraved in stone. The varieties he names are merely suggestions. "It's hard to have a garden be all things to all people," he says, "but there's a lot of leeway in this for them to tune in to their own tastes and substitute to their heart's delight."

PLANT	BLOOM	COLOR	HEIGHT
Alyssum (annual)	June–Sept.	white	3–4 in.
Artemisia 'Silver King'	foliage only	gray	2–3 ft.
Aster x frikartii	June–Sept.	lavender	3 ft.
Astilbe (tall variety)	June–July	deep pink	3–4 ft.
Baby's breath (Gypsophila reptens)	June–Aug.	white or pale pink	6 in.
Bleeding heart (Dicentra spectabilis)	May–June	pink	2 ft.
Campanula carpatica	June–Sept.	blue	8 in.
Catmint (Nepeta mussinii)	June–Aug.	gray-green foliage	18 in.
Columbine (Aquilegia)	May–June	yellow	2 ft.
Cosmos (annual, tall variety)	Aug.–Sept.	white	4 ft.
Cranesbill (Geranium) 'Johnson's Blue'	June–Sept.	lavender blue	4 ft.
Dahlia (annual)	June–Sept.	crimson	5 ft.
Damask rose 'Quatre Saisons'	June & Sept.	pale pink	4 ft.
Daylily (Hemerocallis) 'Catherine Woodbury'	June–Aug.	lavender pink	2 ft.
Globe thistle (Echinops)	June–Sept.	steel blue	15 in.
Hollyhock (old-fashioned single)	June–Sept.	deep pink	4–5 ft.
Iris (tall bearded)	May–June	white & yelllow	3 ft.
Iris (Siberian)	June–July	deep purple	3 ft.
Lupine	June–July	deep blue	3–5 ft.
Maiden pink (Dianthus deltoides)	May–June	pink	4–6 in.
Meadowsweet (Filipendula) 'Queen of the Prairie'	June–July	white	4 ft.
Monkshood (Aconitum fischeri)	Sept.–Oct.	dark blue	4–5 ft.
Pearly everlasting (Anaphalis)	July–Sept.	white	2 ft.
Peony 'Alice Harding"	May–June	pink	3 ft.
Peony 'Miss America'	May–June	white	3 ft.
Phlox 'Mt. Fuji'	July–Sept.	white	3 ft.
Poppy (Orientale)	June	scarlet	3–4 ft.
Pot marigold (Calendula)	Aug.–Oct.	peachy	2 ft.
Sedum 'Autumn Joy'	Aug.–Sept.	rusty pink	2 ft.
Snapdragon	July–Sept.	burgundy	2 ft.
Snakeroot (Cimicifuga)	July–Aug.	white	6 ft.
Sundrops (evening primrose)	June–Aug.	yellow	18 in.
Sweet pea (grown on brush)	June–Sept.	pink & red	2–3 ft.
Tiger lily	July–Aug.	orange	3–5 ft.
Viola	May–Sept.	sky blue	6 in.
Yarrow (Achillea millefolium) 'Moonshine'	June–Sept.	yellow	18–24 in.

The Cottage Garden

With the exception of those which focus on one particular species, most Maine gardens, whether developed by creative home gardeners or designed by such luminaries as Beatrix Farrand and Patrick Chassé, fall into the category of "cottage garden." The introduction I wrote for the program of the 1991 Maine State Horticultural Show, published as a Down East *supplement, explains it all.*

Ask ten gardeners what a cottage garden is and you're likely to get ten different definitions—definitions as diverse and colorful as the many different blooms that can be found in gardens across the length and breadth of Maine.

A cottage garden can be the informal collection that many of us remember around Grandmother's doorstep, a charming profusion of bright spring bulbs and lush, heavy-scented peonies, followed later by sunny golden glow, scarlet bee balm, blue delphiniums, and pink rambling roses—plants whose origin, if remembered at all, was a friend or neighbor's garden, plants that have been divided and shared in their turn.

At the other end of the spectrum are the "cottage gardens" that embellish the homes of the affluent, gardens whose noble lineage can be traced to the landscape architect's drawing board and the commercial nursery, and whose sophisticated glory adorns the pages of glossy magazines.

"The thing about having a cottage garden that's so wonderful," says Nancy Jackson, a Rockport gardener and profes-

> *Originally a garden enclosure was a haven from the wild heath or forest without.*

sional garden designer, "is that you can put anything into it that you want—the things you really love—with no constraints as to color or plant material." Interestingly, when Jackson designs a garden for someone else, she's very careful about colors and textures, a clear example of the cottage garden's flexible parameters.

"A nice, romantic, old-fashioned garden" is what Mamie Ney of the Junior League of Portland says league members were looking for when they chose "A Maine Cottage Garden" as this year's theme. The definition they followed came from the July 1990 issue of *House Beautiful*: "A lovely, enclosed world to linger in . . . [which] also supplies food and cutting flowers." Some sort of enclosure—a fence, a wall, a hedge, the angle of a building—is traditional. Originally a garden enclosure was a haven from the wild heath or forest without; nowadays it provides a peaceful refuge from the hustle and bustle of the outside world.

Cottage gardens, "those neatly kept and productive little gardens round the laborers' houses, which are seldom unornamented with more or less of flowers" (William Cobbett's definition from the 1820s), are generally thought to have originated in fifteenth- or sixteenth-century England, when "nosegaie gardens" introduced flowers to the largely herbal gardens of the Middle Ages and when vegetables were becoming accepted as food for people rather than just for livestock. Shakespeare's "gilly-flowers" (clove pinks), "cuckoo buds" (buttercups), roses, lilies, and "marigolds" (calendulas) were among the favorites. W. H. Hudson described these gardens in 1910 as having "the old, homely, cottage garden blooms, so old that they have entered the soul." The English cottage garden (as Cobbett defined it) persists today, as any traveler can attest who has admired the tiny, flower-filled plots that still abound in English manufacturing towns and country villages.

It may come as a surprise that New England's "old-fashioned" gardens are not direct descendants of the English cottage garden. The replicas of early American gardens at Old Sturbridge Village are devoted to culinary and medicinal herbs but contain few flowers, perhaps reflecting Yankee austerity. Nor do the reproduction eighteenth-century gardens of Williamsburg and Monticello draw their inspiration from traditional folk gardens; they are instead patterned after the formal, stylized gardens that set off the English great houses of the period.

However, it was the English cottage gardens, their narrow confines crowded with flowers, vegetables, and fruit trees, that inspired a revolution in landscape design in the late nineteenth century. The English garden designer Gertrude Jekyll proclaimed that flowers should be planted in colorful drifts rather than neatly spaced, formal patterns. Jekyll's "natural" look was later carried to elegant heights in such famous English estate

NANCE TRUEWORTHY

Some sort of enclosure is traditional for a cottage garden.

gardens as Sissinghurst and Hidcote. American landscape architect Beatrix Farrand, who studied with Jekyll, brought her ideas to this country to create the celebrated gardens of Dumbarton Oaks in Washington, D.C., as well as several in the Maine town of Bar Harbor, where she summered. A fine example of Farrand's sophisticated "cottage gardens" is The Farm House Garden in Bar Harbor, with its exuberantly blooming borders restored by Betsy Moore.

Only in the past ten years or so have Americans begun to abandon the stiff rows of tulips and marigolds and the clipped evergreens, and wholeheartedly embraced the English cottage-gardening style. In Maine, the previously small catalog of available blooms, such as the old-fashioned perennials planted around grandmother's doorstep and the standard annuals bought by the flat each spring, has expanded exponentially to include dozens of new varieties as well as many of the old, long-forgotten ones. The scope of these "old-fashioned" gardens has also changed; the whole mix now fills, in some cases, the entire space between front gate and front door.

The criteria for a well-planned cottage garden include unconscious elegance, a lack of artifice, and a sense of harmony with nature. But the basic tenet remains individual taste, both in design (or lack of it) and content. One authority endorses the "tangled" effect; another insists that to define cottage gardens as formless jumbles is misleading, because traditionally not an inch was wasted in these small spaces where much of the family food was raised. Whichever definition he or she fancies,

The colors of stone and lichen blend naturally with the mix of blooms in this cottage garden.

The Grand Masters of Maine Gardening

independent cottage gardener can choose to let color run riot, joyfully juxtaposing an orange poppy with a magenta blazing star, or can limit the palette to delicate, cool shades of pink or blue.

There are those who insist that a cottage garden isn't a cottage garden without at least one old-fashioned rose, delphinium (or its easier-to-grow annual cousin, the larkspur), calendula, Canterbury bell, and hollyhock. A purist might restrict the garden's contents to heirloom plants, available only from specialty houses. One gardener might concentrate on herbs such as dill, fennel, lavender, rosemary, thyme, rue, and sage, while another may succumb to every temptation in the seed catalog. Vegetables are traditional cottage-garden ingredients and are more fun to grow among flowers than in standard rows, though here again, individual treatment varies from pleasant orderliness to charming abandon. Honeysuckles frequently clamber over a fence or a windowside trellis, whence their fragrance wafts indoors on a summer afternoon. Equally welcome are berry bushes and fruit trees, or sa stand of rhubarb for an early spring tonic.

Maine cottage gardeners might find a more appropriate guide in Celia Thaxter's Victorian flower garden on Appledore Island in the Isles of Shoals. The garden has been restored recently and is maintained by a New Hampshire garden club. In her book *An Island Garden*, first published in 1893 and once again

LYNN KARLIN

Single hollyhocks. Great-grandmother's tried-and-true flowers still grace Maine's dooryards.

in print, Thaxter lovingly describes cultivating more than a hundred varieties of flowers in the decidedly less than ideal growing climate of her island home.

Whether one chooses to follow tradition —and books on the subject abound—or one's own fancy, the cottage garden remains an intimate, creative, personal adornment of the place called home.

Celia Thaxter's
Victorian Garden

Perhaps the archetypal Maine cottage garden was created by Celia Thaxter, a popular poet of the 1890s, on Appledore Island, where her family operated a summer hotel. Thaxter's garden differed in some ways from modern cottage gardens. Constant hybridization in the past hundred years has resulted in shorter plant material along with the loss of old stock, making it difficult to authentically replicate her tall Victorian garden. In 2002, Virginia Chisholm and her associate, Marjorie Duquenne, celebrated their twentieth year of caring for the garden and guiding visitors. Admission fees during that time have raised $100,000 for undergraduate scholarships to the Shoals Marine Laboratory's program, Duquenne reported. The garden is open from June to the end of August. See Appendix for more information.

A hundred years ago, one of Maine's most admired gardens, a colorful riot of poppies, hollyhocks, sweet peas, and other Victorian favorites, flourished about ten miles offshore from Kittery, Maine, on Appledore Island in the Isles of Shoals. It was the cherished creation of Celia Thaxter, a popular poet of the day and a writer whose descriptive prose appeared in such respected periodicals as *The Atlantic Monthly*. Today, Celia Thaxter is not mentioned in even the most comprehensive anthologies of American literature, but her last work, an enchanting little volume called *An Island Garden*, may well serve to perpetuate both her name and her garden. It was written at the urging of her many literary and artistic friends, who vacationed at the famous Appledore Hotel and were charmed by her small oasis of flowers and greenery. They included such luminaries as James Russell Lowell, Nathaniel Hawthorne, William Dean Howells, and American Impressionist Childe Hassam, whose paintings illustrated her book.

An Island Garden, repeatedly in and out of print, has become a minor classic among New England gardeners and has served as a blueprint for the restoration of the garden itself, which is once again drawing visitors to "the low, bleached rocks of the Isles of Shoals." [Houghton Mifflin, the original publisher, brought out a $35 slipcased edition of *An Island Garden* in 2001; it is the only version now in print.]

Today's garden lacks the setting that would be recognized by one-time Shoalers (as the summer regulars were called)—a fenced-in terrace in front of the long piazza of a substantial two-story "cottage." The cottage was one of a number of summer residences on the island owned by Celia's family, who operated the huge, rambling Appledore Hotel. The hotel and many of the cottages were destroyed by fire in 1914. Now the only occupant of Appledore Island is the Shoals Marine Laboratory, a joint venture of the University of New Hampshire and Cornell University.

Dr. John Kingsbury, the laboratory's

former director, now retired, was fascinated by the Thaxter legend, which still persists on the islands. Reviving Celia's long-lost garden became a welcome diversion from microscopes and computers for Dr. Kingsbury, his staff, and students. With the aid of a backhoe and a rototiller, they began in 1977 to restore the site, well marked by the old cottage foundation but overgrown with wild cherry, sumac, and witchgrass. Their guide was Celia's book, written the year before her death in 1894.

The hobby soon outgrew the spare time and financial resources of the marine laboratory enthusiasts. To help support the project, Dr. Kingsbury published a new hardcover edition of *An Island Garden* in 1978 and began giving lectures. The interest he aroused brought aid from many sources, including the Little Boars Head Garden Club of North Hampton, New Hampshire, and the Driftwood Garden Club of Rye, New Hampshire.

The latter now takes care of the restored garden for the marine laboratory.

The Isles of Shoals, a group of nine small islands ten miles offshore, are divided by the Maine–New Hampshire state line. White Island, where Celia went to live at the age of four when her father became the lighthouse keeper, and Star Island, now noted as a conference center, are in New Hampshire, along with two others. Appledore, the largest of the islands, and another four are in Maine. Celia moved with her family to Appledore in 1848, when her father, Thomas Laighton, built the Appledore Hotel, and continued to live there year-round until her marriage, at sixteen, to Levi Thaxter. She returned to the island in summer throughout her life to help at the hotel and in winter to visit or nurse her aging parents, but other responsibilities often kept her on the mainland.

Contrary to the impression given by her

Gardens she had seen in Europe may have inspired Celia to build the raised beds for her island garden.

Poppies were among Celia Thaxter's favorite flowers.

NANCE TRUEWORTHY

tances, but some, including John Greenleaf Whittier; James T. Fields, editor of *The Atlantic*, and his wife, Annie; and Sarah Orne Jewett, were among Celia's dearest friends. As one guest explained, she held "a sort of salon mornings and evenings." Arriving by her garden gate, climbing her front steps, and crossing the vine-shaded piazza, visitors then entered a room filled with paintings, photographs, usually music, and always flowers. One morning a friend counted 110 vases!

It was to supply these vases and to nourish her passion for natural beauty that Celia kept her garden. She had planted her first garden, a yard-square plot of pot marigolds (calendulas), on barren White Island when she was no more than five years old. Later, on Appledore, where the wind-stunted vegetation seemed luxuriant to her twelve-year-old eyes, she grew marigolds and flax, the latter so that she could see the color of the eyes of the captain's daughter in Longfellow's "The Wreck of the Hesperus." Flowers and poetry were inseparable in her mind long before they came together in her parlor. Her own words, lush with a Victorian ardor almost embarrassing to modern ears, capture the symbiosis of parlor and garden: "Year after year a long procession of charming people come and go within [the parlor's] doors, and the flowers that glow for their delight seem to listen with them to the music that stirs each blossom upon its stem." Every morning, sometimes as early as four o'clock, Celia would "go forth" to tend her garden and cut masses of bloom for the house. Plants of every available variety that she could coax to grow in the island's trying climate overhung the garden's narrow footpaths.

Although she took care to plant tall growers along the fences and made sure the shorter ones had their share of sunlight and air, landscape gardening was not her aim. Her

book (deliberately, for she was even more reticent about her personal trials than the average New Englander), Celia was not a lady of leisure who wrote for her own amusement. She was a gifted writer and artist who supported herself largely through her talents in time stolen from household drudgery and family cares. Though no specific date is known for her garden's beginning, Celia was able to give it increasing attention during the last ten years of her life, after her husband's death in 1884. It is this period that she describes in *An Island Garden*.

Long before this time, however, visitors to the island had been welcomed in Celia's parlor. There were plenty of mere acquain-

landscape was the natural world around her. One August day she wrote in her diary: "Outside the garden this tranquil morning the soft green turf that slopes smoothly to the sea in front is shaggy with thick dew from which the yet low sun strikes a thousand broken rainbows. The clumps of wild Roses glow with their red haws in the full light; the Elder bushes are laden with clusters of purple berries; Goldenrod and wild Asters bloom, and a touch of fire begins to light up the Huckleberry bushes . . . The gray rocks show so fair in the changing lights, and all the dear island with its sights and sounds is set in the pale light summer-blue of a smiling sea as if it were June, with hardly a wave to break its happy calm. The same ashes-of-roses color as that which makes lovely the skies of May holds the fair world in a light embrace. . . . Though the tide is full, it makes no murmur."

Heady as *An Island Garden* is with such effulgent prose, the book is also, as Dr. Kingsbury remarks in his introduction, "practical to a surprising degree in a work of literary quality." This he attributes to Celia's "lifetime of acute nature observation at the Shoals, unceasing experimentation, and nurturing growing things." Some of Celia's practices may seem quaint in the light of a century of horticultural progress. Her arsenal against the garden's insect foes included hellebore, yellow snuff, lime, salt, Paris green, cayenne pepper, kerosene emulsion, and whale-oil soap. For the cutworms that destroyed her beloved sweet peas, she found "no remedy so sure as seeking a personal interview and slaying them on the spot." On the other hand, we are still using much the same weapons as Celia did against the loathsome slug. She surrounded plants with rings of ashes or air-slaked lime, used little cages of fine wire netting over some, or filled wooden troughs around the beds with salt. Her ultimate, and apparently successful, solution to slugs was to import toads. "If there is one thing I love more than another," she wrote to her friend Annie Fields, "it is a toad."

Each spring she had to defend her newly sown seeds from armies of migrating songbirds and the song sparrows that came to stay for the summer. Nothing but heavy planks laid over the rows until the seeds germinated deterred the "merry little marauders," as she called them. All the familiar weeds Celia had in abundance, but her special affliction was dodder, a wild island plant that got into her garden by accident. A parasite, it strangles every plant that comes within its grasp. Weeding gave her as much pleasure as every other garden chore. (She did them all, except for the initial spring spading, herself.) She would put two boards down near the plot she had to weed, spread a piece of carpet on them, and sit or lie with her face as close to the work as possible.

Celia prepared for her spring garden in the fall. She gathered seedpods of annuals and used their dry stalks to mulch perennials. She scattered fine barn manure over the perennials, adding wood ashes around the clematis, honeysuckle, grapevines, and roses. This would be worked into the ground in the spring. "I have never found anything to equal barn manure as food for flowers," she wrote. Luckily there were cows and horses on the island to supply the hotel with milk and transportation. She would have several cartloads of manure piled near her garden in the autumn to be "rendered fit" by the elements for use the following spring. She also kept a compost heap for use on flowers that do not like barn manure. "Keep barn manure away from your Lilies for your life!" she admonished.

The instinctive green thumb Celia was said to have inherited from her mother, her intense scientific curiosity, and years of prac-

Sparse soil and strong winds are still the two major challenges for anyone attempting to garden on the Isles of Shoals.

tical experience made her a skilled amateur horticulturist. In a time when commercial seed packaging was relatively primitive, she observed that a seedsman could make a fortune by printing each plant's requirements right on the seed packet, a hint that has obviously been followed, with the predicted results. She even suggested appropriate copy: "Why not say of Mignonette, It flourishes best in a poor and sandy soil; so treated, it is much more fragrant than in rich earth.... Or of Pansies, Give them the richest earth you can find, no end of water, and partial shade...."

In *An Island Garden*, Celia described the habits, problems, and most particularly the beauties of more than a hundred species of cultivated plants. Many of them were annuals, and many of these she started in flats in January, following much the same procedures that modern commercial growers use. Lacking today's peat pots and compartmentalized flats, she grew her poppies and other plants that are difficult to transplant in eggshells, which she provided with drainage holes at the bottom and set in boxes of sand. These could then be set out without disturbing the roots by merely breaking away the shell. "This pleasant business goes on during the winter in the picturesque old town of Portsmouth, New Hampshire, whither I repair in the autumn... returning to the islands on the first of April," she wrote. "My upper windows all winter are

The Grand Masters of Maine Gardening

filled with young Wallflowers, Stocks, Poppies and many other garden plants . . . till the time comes for transporting them over the seas to Appledore. A small steam tug, the *Pinafore,* carries me and my household belongings over to the islands, and a pretty sight is the little vessel when she starts out from the old brown wharves and steams away down the beautiful Piscataqua River, with her hurricane deck awave with green leaves and flowers, for all the world like a May Day procession."

Every plant was precious to Celia Thaxter and each individual blossom a minor miracle. She advised carrying a magnifying glass into the garden, the better to discover the subtlety and "wealth of ornament" reflected in even

the smallest blossom. She delighted in the scents and loved nothing better than a blaze of color, especially the oranges and yellows of calendulas and California poppies. But she was also partial to white, planting white petunias, poppies, and nicotiana "because they were so beautiful by moonlight." No flower is mentioned without affection, but it would be safe to say that her favorites were sweet peas and poppies, judging from the amount of effort she devoted to raising them and the space they occupy in her book. There was no horticultural adventure that Celia would not attempt. She even grew water lilies and lotuses in tubs. How she would have gloried in the seed and nursery catalogs we have today!

Replicating Celia Thaxter's garden has proved more challenging but no less enjoyable than Dr. Kingsbury anticipated, according to Virginia Chisholm of the Driftwood Garden Club. Mrs. Chisholm has been in charge of the garden's care for the past several years. Finding the plants Celia used required a great deal of research, begun by Dr. Kingsbury and his daughter and continued by Mrs. Chisholm. She has been able to locate sources for most of the plants, but in many cases the modern hybrids are much shorter. She is troubled by not being able to reproduce Celia's "high Victorian garden."

"It took us a long time to figure out that middle bed," says Mrs. Chisholm. The diagram Celia drew, perhaps in haste, includes only a small portion of the many plants she mentioned in her text. "She had her own name for things. She listed on her map Crimson Phlox, but I knew it wouldn't go with what she had planned in that bed. It turned out to be red *flax*. I'd never seen it, but it's perfectly beautiful." Celia did indeed call it Crimson Flax in her text, but apparently an error crept into the map.

All manner of catalogs, American and English, were consulted in the search for specific old varieties. To reestablish Celia's old-fashioned roses, Mrs. Chisholm sent to a firm in California that specializes in heirloom plants. "We also have a little old Scotch rose that somebody gave me from a cemetery in Rye," she notes. The only place she was able to find the sunflowers Celia fancied was at the Hamilton House, in South Berwick, another historic garden that Mrs. Chisholm takes care of. "I went around and gathered hollyhock seeds and old nicotiana seeds in the

One morning a visiting friend counted 110 vases of flowers in Celia's parlor.

gardens of my friends," she continues. "The new nitcotianas are only about eighteen inches high and have no aroma, you know. A friend from Kittery brought me hesperis [sweet rocket] to put in the corners as Celia did. And it was actually a legacy from Celia. She had given it to my friend's mother, I think. That was fun to get."

Mrs. Chisholm found Celia's wisteria, Japanese hops, and akebia vines overgrowing their original surroundings. "Her clematis, much like the modern *Clematis paniculata*, is all over the island," Mrs. Chisholm reports. "The birds have seeded it. But it isn't in the garden. Last year I found a whole bower of it." Attempts at propagating and replanting the clematis are still in the trial stage. There is some possibility of restoring Celia's porch as a sort of free-standing pavilion to accommodate the vines and provide a shady picnic spot for visitors.

"This is a marvelous garden, and Celia was very clever in designing it," says Mrs. Chisholm, who is a veritable encyclopedia of Thaxter lore. "Of course, she'd been to Europe and she'd probably seen raised beds there, because when she came back she planned this. It's the easiest garden to take care of." There have been problems, but not the same ones Celia faced. The soil is poor without the plentiful supplies of manure. Seaweed is a fair substitute, but it has to be gathered on nearby Sandpiper Beach after a storm. Soil to rebuild the beds must be brought from the mainland. Fortunately, the slugs have disappeared, and insect pests appear to be minimal, except for hordes of red ants. Although they do the garden no harm, they put Celia's horizontal weeding style out of the question, Mrs. Chisholm remarks dryly.

Muskrats, an accidental import, are rampant on the islands. The garden is fenced with boards, to break the strong winds, and chicken wire, which is buried a foot deep. Still, the muskrats burrow in, and precious soil is washed out through their tunnels in heavy rains. Gulls, which were infrequent visitors in Celia's day, have colonized the islands. They make a game of pulling up young plants. They also, indirectly, limit the water supply. In Appledore's heyday, hotel and cottages were plentifully supplied with rainwater collected from roofs and stored in cisterns, making it possible for Celia to hose down her garden in dry weather and to cultivate exotics such as waterlilies. With gulls now crowding every ridgepole, collecting rainwater from the roofs is no longer even contemplated.

Water lilies are not the only item on Celia Thaxter's list that has not reappeared. So far, Mrs. Chisholm has been unable to locate the tall, single dahlias that Celia always raised from seed or the white poppy she prized so highly. But she expects that one day the project will be completed.

In keeping with the garden's tradition, seedlings are raised on the mainland, some by Mrs. Chisholm in her own greenhouse, but mostly by Chris Robarge, head of the greenhouses at the Thompson School of Agriculture at the University of New Hampshire, in Durham.

Interest in Celia Thaxter's garden continues to grow. Not only garden clubs but other nature-oriented groups visit on tours. Yachts stop by. Passengers from the *Viking Sun*, which runs excursion trips from Portsmouth to Star Island, are frequent visitors. Many people have volunteered to come out and help with the garden, which is maintained by marine lab students between Mrs. Chisholm's weekly visits. What would be the greatest help of all, she says with a staunch New England practicality that Celia surely would have seconded, is for everyone who comes to Appledore Island to bring along a bag of soil.

Nellie Davis Stops Traffic at Bean's Corner

If the true cottage garden is one that fills every inch of the yard, Nellie Davis has achieved it. Still gardening at eighty-four, she admitted to feeling only "passable," and reluctantly reported that her garden is now smaller than the one I saw in 1998. The quiet Bean's Corner crossing has been "improved" with a blinking light, but the traffic speeding by slows less frequently to glimpse the show. Nellie now visits her husband, Albert, in a nursing home. But her indomitable spirit is unchanged. She is equally moved by the sight of her peonies in bloom and by the generous help she receives from friends. No matter what, "you can always find a blessing," she says, her voice as cheery as ever.

You can talk about your elegant estate gardens along the Maine Coast, your unique historical treasures like Celia Thaxter's island garden, your spectacular displays of azaleas or lilacs or delphiniums, but there's probably no garden anywhere in Maine that gives so much downright, everyday delight as the one that stops traffic all summer long at Bean's Corner in North Jay.

From rainbow ribbons of deep purple dwarf iris and pink creeping phlox in June to the autumn bonfire of gloriosa daisies and late-blooming calendulas, every inch of this roadside-backyard garden, on a high ridge that looks westward to the rolling blue hills of Farmington and the mountains beyond, overflows with color. Chance passersby are dazzled and, often as not, stop for a closer look. Longtime admirers return year after year. And once they get acquainted with her, it's the gardener herself as much as her work of art they come to see.

A slight, frail-looking woman, Nellie Davis greets a visitor in a voice as clear and vibrant as a schoolgirl's. "Just walk around and enjoy the garden, and don't forget to sign the guest book. It's in the mailbox at the top of the path." Her snapping dark eyes, under the brim of her becoming—but practical—straw garden hat, complete the aura of youthful charm that somehow seems not at all incongruous with her seventy-nine years. Welcome to Lornell Gardens, named for the Lord and Nellie, she explains. The Lord has provided her with a long succession of blessings and challenges, but it's Nellie herself who has made the most of them with her love of beauty, her eagerness to experiment, and her tireless dedication to her garden.

"I garden for health of body, mind, and soul," she declares as she leads the way through the garden, despite her admonition that she's busy and you're on your own. An intuitive teacher, she just can't help conducting the tour. For the body, she recommends the exercise that gardening affords and the nutritional advantages of growing your own vegetables (which share considerable space with her flowers). For the mind, there's nothing as stimulating as trying something new, she maintains. For the soul, it's the flowers. "It's exciting to be able to work in a pretty place," she says, "and healthy, too. You need to do something for the world. A lot of people have told me, time and again, how much they enjoy going by here." Signatures and comments in her guest book, as many as four hundred one summer, are sufficient testimony. Photographer Kevin Shields was so entranced that he made four trips to Bean's Corner for this story, Nellie relates with pleasure. She felt especially honored by one caller last summer, a photographer for *National Geographic*. How did he know about her? she asked him. "I was just driving by and put on the brakes," he said.

Nellie loves to tell the story of her garden's evolution and has an anecdote for every trick she's learned in the process. She and her husband, Albert, moved to North Jay twenty-six years ago when he was transferred from a job in New Hampshire. It was the first place she'd had room enough for a real garden. "I didn't know much about it at the time, but I kept learning. The more I know, the more there is to learn," she says. She began raising herbs, surprising her father when he visited her. "Do you know what you've got there?" he asked her excitedly. "Yes, I planted it," she replied. "I used to pick that for my mother," he told her. Nellie's grandmother had been the town herbalist in a Lithuanian village.

Nellie definitely sees the hand of the Lord in the long, flower-covered mound that runs like a spine down her garden's center. "I had a nice little garden, all ready for winter," she relates, "and the septic system quit. Come to find out, it was just a small hole in the ground. We had to have a new septic system, so this hill is my septic system." Much of her garden, lovingly built over the years, had to be destroyed to construct the leach field, but Nellie was undaunted. "I know why it happened. The Lord wanted me to have a beautiful garden

Nellie Davis with her superb gloriosa daisies (Rudbeckia hirta).

there. [The contractor] told me to plant grass or flowers, but I wasn't going to plant grass to mow, so I stuck to flowers. It cost me eight thousand dollars to have that mound built. They had to bring in a lot of soil. But it actually makes it prettier." It's the height of the mound that creates the grand display visible from the road, showing off early spring bulbs, daffodils and narcissus, peonies, irises and lilies, lupines, clematis and delphinium, and the multicolored tapestry of late summer.

The deep ditch behind the mound is part of a drainage system Nellie created to divert the spring runoff from her neighbor's land above. At first the loose sand of the fill kept sliding into the ditch. She knew she needed the drainage, and her husband had had an operation and couldn't help her dig it out. "I was digging sand and shoveling water. Did you ever shovel water? It's a dreadful job, and the sand kept coming down." She solved the problem by planting the whole bank with pulmonaria (lungwort). Contrary to its shade-loving nature, it thrives there in full sun, along with an unusual bedfellow, hens and chickens, which loves sun and sandy soil.

But Nellie isn't deterred by what ought to be. She just follows her own inclination, and if it works, fine. If not, she goes on to something else. She's justifiably proud of her ingenuity. "Come down here and look at my squashes," she invites. The sturdy, foot-high plants are well ahead of any squash planted by ordinary methods, but because of the very cold spring, Nellie says, hers haven't achieved their usual three-foot June growth. She likes her winter squash good and ripe, so she contrived a way to outsmart the short growing season in Maine's western foothills. Glass gallon jugs squat near the squash bed, as well as all over the garden, awaiting storage now that they've served their springtime purpose. With the bottoms cut out (one of Albert's jobs), they are perfect cloches for seedlings, vegetables and flowers alike. Under them, Nellie sets out broccoli in March, squash in late April. "In early May, when they expected a freeze, I even put a styrofoam cup over the tiny seedling, then the jug over that, so they survived," she says. The caps hang by a wire to the jug handle, ready to seal in the heat when the sun goes down and come off for ventilation during the day.

> *"I garden for health of body, mind, and soul."*

Nellie has tried chicken wire laid flat to deter slugs, has found that aluminum flashing bent to extend over the lawn works better than the usual vertical edging to keep grass out of flower beds, and keeps a shaker with large holes handy for sowing carrot seeds. She irrigates an individual plant by sinking a clay flower pot with a hole in the bottom beside it and filling the pot with water. "When you water the plant, instead of the water running all over, it goes down to the root where it belongs," she says. Reflecting on her problem solving, she adds, "So I struggle, not to be smart or beat anybody, just trying to do the best I can for myself. And I'm always willing to tell everybody what I do and why I do it."

Compost, which Nellie and Albert make in small piles and don't bother to turn, is probably the most important ingredient in the rich soil that has been built up from heavy clay over the years. Most of the raised beds that fill the entire lot are divided by weedless pathways of sawdust or wood shavings. When this covering gets old and decayed, it goes into the adjacent beds and is replaced with a fresh lot. Compost also figures in one of Nellie's favorite stories. A neighbor, now deceased, offered her some extra space in his garden. She planted her beans right beside his bean row. Hers flourished, but his did not. "I tell you, I was kind of embarrassed," she relates with a smile, "but the thing of it was, I used compost and cow manure and mulch, and he didn't. I guess he didn't want to copy an old lady, but he found out those things were working. He finally decided to use mulch."

Lornell Garden's rich soil nourishes a multitude of flora, from the ordinary to the exotic—from sunny calendulas that put on such a fall show, Nellie says, because she cuts back the first spent bloom in August, to the patch of yellow lady's slippers beside the

Calendula and nigella. Bold, bright color fills every inch of Nellie's roadside garden.

Nellie Davis Stops Traffic at Bean's Corner   ❧ 65

house, which she has kept going for almost twenty-five years. Oddly enough, there are almost no roses. Perhaps because of the richness of the soil, they became so rampant that she couldn't control them. "Nothing stopped them, so I stopped selling them," she says. Although she doesn't raise things just to sell, she often has surpluses that can be purchased, either as plant divisions or as cut flowers, especially in the wedding season. Last year she cut three hundred stems of irises.

One thing that regular visitors will miss this year is the huge stand of tall red phlox that has long been a highlight of the late summer. Nellie suddenly discovered she was intensely allergic to the blossoms, and even had to have someone else dig them up. But the gap was quickly filled with a fantastic spread of gloriosa daisies, which seed themselves every year, reaffirming her belief that this is the Lord's garden. "God put his hand in and created this wild, gorgeous mass of daisies," she insists. One strong testimony to Nellie's unshaking faith is that a woman who has had serious health problems all her life has been able to maintain this small Eden. Along with a variety of ailments, she is allergic to a long list of foods and flowers, but she continues to research alternative medicine and find ways to circumvent what in her case are hard to call handicaps. Much of the season she has to wear a mask to work in the garden. She grows (all organically) only the vegetables that she is able to eat, which eliminates many of the most common ones.

What is not missing is Nellie's indomitable sense of humor. As to her minimal amount of lawn, she says, "I follow the European method. In Europe, people don't have lawns. They have nice flower gardens. It's a waste of space to have just lawn to put Roundup on. In fact, I'm the 'roundup kid'— I go around rounding up all the neighbors' dandelions!" She cans and freezes these "extremely healthy" wild greens, which she is surprised more people don't take advantage of. "When you have something beautiful, you should use it," she says.

Nellie follows the time-honored method of cooking dandelion greens in several changes of water but, she says, "It's wise to get used to a little bit of bitter, because the Lord gave us all the senses for our taste—bitter, sweet, sour, salt—and if we don't get a little bit of each flavor, we don't feel satisfied." Despite her health concerns, Nellie Davis finds life satisfying in many ways. Even in winter, she stays in touch with her garden, making exquisite note cards with the flowers she presses during the summer, using everything from tiny forget-me-nots to robust jack-in-the-pulpits.

"I love every facet of nature," says Nellie, who leaves a dead shrub in place because it's "the birds' airport" on their way to the feeders, puts out string for nesting orioles, and welcomes swallows as substitute tenants in her bluebird houses. "I like going out to pick wild mushrooms in the fall. I like this flower bed where the birdbath is. The dianthus will be all pink and the middle will be all yellow evening primrose. That's a sight! I work here almost day and night, but we live so far from all our friends and relatives that it's a good thing we've got something to keep us happy. And I have all these people who come back every year to see me in the garden. That makes life interesting."

Bernard Etzel,
Farmington's Master Gardener

Though he has had to furl the banner of phlox that festooned his hillside lawn when I visited him in 1995, Bing Etzel is still welcoming visitors, still advising garden clubs, still teaching, still hiking the mountains, still expanding his fern collection, which now contains forty-five of Maine's fifty native species. College students and botanical societies from around New England come to admire and learn about the most complete fern garden in Maine. As he looks around Farmington, Etzel sees everywhere the evidence of his fifty years of promoting interest in gardening. "It's a joy to see so many people growing flowers," he says.

A brilliant banner of phlox in every shade from pale pink to deep magenta, streaming down the grassy slope from a big, white Victorian house, proclaims Bernard ("Bing") Etzel's love for color. "Everything [I do] is for color," says the lean, well-tanned gardener, who's been developing this showplace near downtown Farmington for more than forty years. "A lot of people have what I call a collection of plants. They have a lot of different things, but if I like something, I have millions of them."

Masses of blue forget-me-nots accented by red and yellow tulips headed Etzel's season-long color parade in May. In June, peonies began to fill in the background along with hundreds of foxgloves and Canterbury bells, while a profusion of pink and white sweet william took over from the forget-me-nots. Poppies, lilies, five-foot-tall McKana hybrid columbine, and giant blue delphinium moved the procession along, and by mid-July the phlox were beginning to assert themselves.

"Right up into August, I have no problem having lots of color," Etzel says. "This is ablaze with phlox right up to the house, the highest color of the year. The problem is that most garden phlox are all done by mid-August." A constant experimenter, with a degree in horticulture from the University of Maine in the 1940s, Etzel has discovered a way around this annoyance. "I found several [phlox] plants that flowered late, a lavender and a pink. I waited till the second year, and they did the same thing. I took those plants and spread them all out in the growing bed. I've been running tests for three or four years, getting bigger plants. Now I've put them into the regular garden, and I'll have lavender and pink during the last part of August." Because Etzel and his wife, Elizabeth, leave in October for their winter home in Florida, he doesn't want to spend time with late-blooming plants such as chrysanthemums and asters.

Although the spectacular border is the first thing that catches the eye of passersby on the steep street, it isn't the only attraction of the Etzel demesne. In spring, a magnificent star magnolia takes center stage in the lawn, dwarfed only by a strong contender for the "Biggest Sugar Maple" prize in the town's bicentennial celebration last year. Dense plantings of rose and white impatiens surround the lovingly tended trees and follow the contours of the house's old-fashioned wraparound porch, where baskets of fuchsia hang, to the delight of both the hummingbirds and the Etzels, lifelong bird lovers. Tubs overflowing with petunias mark the porch steps. Everywhere, less showy but no less lovely plants reward a closer look—pulmonaria, *Trollius* (globe flower, sometimes called double buttercup), bleeding heart, Virginia bluebells, and many more in their season.

The path to Bernard Etzel's woods garden

KEVIN SHIELDS

To satisfy his passion for color, Bernard Etzel employs fairly standard garden flowers, grown to well-above-standard luxuriance. But that's only one part of his fascination with horticulture. He's particularly fond of more rare and low-key flora. "The most exciting thing, I think, in gardening is to have a woods garden," he says, eagerly leading the way to a path that angles downward along the side of a deep ravine behind the house. "I go through my gardens several times a day. My happiest moments are with the wildflowers." Etzel makes a point of arriving back in Maine by the end of April to see the woods carpeted with blue scilla as he takes up his season of gardening. Bordering the path, tucked in among the roots of beech and hemlock, surrounding the pond he's built at the bottom of the glen and in the hilltop "bog"—source of the small stream that supplies it—grow gigantic Solomon's seal, jack-in-the pulpit, mayapple, bloodroot, trillium, shooting star, Dutchman's breeches, pink and yellow lady's slipper, skunk cabbage, and marsh marigold, to name a few, along with cultivated woodland plants such as hostas. Most of them are early spring bloomers, and many have come from nurseries that propagate them according to approved methods. "I'm very sensitive to taking a plant in nature where there are only a few," he says. "If I find a place where there are many, I wouldn't hesitate to take a plant here and there."

Ferns—which have no flowers at all—hold a particular enchantment for Etzel. For several years he has been developing a special habitat for them. On a little slope beside the path, chunks of rock from a limestone quarry in Union are set into the soil to create a "limestone cobble." Among them he's planted ferns in soil that's also laced with lime. "The roots will attach themselves to the limerock," he explains. "If I can get them to survive long

The Grand Masters of Maine Gardening

enough to do that, they'll live happily ever after." *Woodsia*, spleenwort, and Braun's holly fern are among the lime-loving ferns. Acid-loving ferns have their own section, and rampant bracken is kept at a safe distance from its more delicate cousins.

As he discusses the technical differences between the evergreen ferns—only one of which is the familiar Christmas fern—and the non-evergreen, the extent of Etzel's horticultural knowledge and his instinct for teaching emerge. "I'm going to have to start labeling them," he says. "People want to know what they are. The botany classes from the college [University of Maine, Farmington] come here to study them. I have close to thirty species of ferns. It took me about four years of wonderful hunting to find them. I had a marvelous time doing it."

Though it looks like virgin forest, Etzel's woodland garden is actually man-made. The area was densely wooded with small trees, which he cleared out, leaving an open understory beneath large timber. He brought in truckloads of woods soil, which he mixed half and half with cow manure. "I have friends with woodlots they were going to clear out and destroy with skidders. They said take all you want. I wasn't stealing anything from nature because it was going to be destroyed anyway," he explains. As much as possible, the surviving plants were lovingly moved to his own gardens. Once Etzel's woodland site was opened up, trout lilies and other wild plants moved into the restored habitat.

Etzel's gardening success rests on well-built soil. "I use compost, all I can make," he says. "I would try to avoid commercial fertilizer, but I can't avoid it with the number of gardens I've got." Three big compost pits lie in a hollow behind a screen of elderberry. One is for succulent material and kitchen waste,

turned several times a summer; one is for leaves, which are left for years until they become black humus; the third is for sod infested with witchgrass and weed seeds. "I want to save the dirt," Etzel observes with typical Yankee thrift. "[That decomposing sod] may be there for a long time, but when I take it out, everything will be dead." There's also a huge pile of cow manure. "I don't think there's anything better than good old cow manure. I buy a couple of truckloads and leave it for six or seven years, covered with black plastic that keeps the weeds down and heats it up." It also prevents water from leaching out the manure's relatively low nutrient content. He uncovers the pile briefly in the rainy season to keep it moist; when it's thoroughly rotted, he runs a small cultivator through it to pulverize the clods.

Compost and manure are the most important nutrients in Etzel's gardens. To these he adds a mixture of 5-10-5 fertilizer and superphosphate, which is 0-44-0. "So I'm really putting on something like 5-25-10," he reckons. He applies fertilizer—sparingly—in spring to give plants a boost. Too much fertilizer causes plants to be spindly, and too much nitrogen causes heavy growth, he says. "You don't want growth, you want flowers! And you need potash for strength of stem." Wood ashes are a good source of potash (potassium) but should be used cautiously to avoid burning. He applies lime every other fall.

Etzel is a great believer in mulch. A thin layer of finely shredded bark keeps down the weeds and reduces the need to water. In the

"Everything I do is for color... If I like something, I have millions of them."

Masses of phlox help provide the color Etzel loves.

course of the season, the mulch works down into the soil as he weeds and cultivates. "That's making soil, really," he says. "It's the expensive way to do it, but if you have as many plants as I have—they run into the thousands—it's a one-man show, and you can't do all the things you'd like to." But beware of what he calls "mulchitis," he says. "If you put on two inches [every year], it builds up and pretty soon the plants are stifled, mulched to death." He mulches as well against the hard winters, running his hands through what's left in the fall

and calculating just how much he needs to add. "I don't ever want more than two inches on it," he says.

Climate is a serious consideration for a Farmington gardener. "We're supposed to be in Zone 4," Etzel says, "but some years, no question we're in Zone 3 [–40 to –20 degrees]." He grows what experience has taught him will usually survive and takes the occasional heavy winter philosophically. He's well versed in strategies for combating the deep freeze and other garden calamities. Tulips he

The Grand Masters of Maine Gardening

plants twelve inches deep on a scoop of bone-meal, much deeper than the level specified for milder climates. He recommends planting lilies in the fall, extra deep and not too early. If they start growing, the sprout may be damaged by frost.

"Our peonies are just getting to be really beautiful," Etzel says, noting that the plants, about eight years old, have by now developed big, tightly packed roots. "They've got to be root-bound to produce good flowers." That gorgeous display of phlox doesn't just happen either. In May, when the shoots are about six inches high, Etzel thins out each plant by about 50 percent, removing any weak-looking stems. "You get more flowers, with bigger heads, and you have less mildew, because the air can filter through the plants."

It's for advice like this, generously offered and seasoned with wry good humor, that people from all over Franklin County come to visit the splendid gardens surrounding the charming hilltop house where Madame Nordica (the famous opera star, born Lillian Norton in Farmington in 1859) once took tea. "This has been our love since 1950," Etzel says, explaining that the place, built in the 1890s by a friend of Nordica's, had fallen on hard times. They purchased it for a song and raised three sons there. Etzel, a native of Freeport, began his "career" in horticulture in college. "I loved it," he recalls, "but I'm not sure it's the best occupation for making a living." After serving in World War II, he planned to go to Cornell for graduate study on the GI Bill, but when he learned that a PhD in horticulture would lead to the princely salary of $2,600 after several years of teaching, he decided to join Elizabeth's father in the family business, Emery's Department Store in Farmington, eventually taking it over. "But I've had my own gardens, my own fun," he says with a grin that hints at the excitement that the thought of gardening always stirs in him.

After retiring in 1971, Etzel needed an outlet for his abundant energy, so he decided to expand his knowledge of birds. He studied ornithology and photography at the University of Maine, Farmington, set up a darkroom, and began lecturing all over the state. He was one of five men featured in a 1973 *Sports Illustrated* article about interesting retirement options and, according to Elizabeth, wore out the magazine's photographers as they followed him around Maine's northwestern woods and streams. Etzel has since given up the exhausting lecture circuit but never his dedication to horticulture. He laid out gardens on both town and county properties in Farmington some twenty years ago and continues as a consultant to the local garden club and other enthusiasts. He recently stepped down as president of the Bonny Woods Association, which is developing sixty-five acres of woodland trails and wildflower habitat as a Farmington public park.

A late spring phone call catches Etzel just returned from collecting ferns in the mountains. "You just lift them out of the leaf mold with your hands, pot them up in compost for a few weeks to get them used to new surroundings, then set them out," he offers enthusiastically, ready as always with an impromptu lesson in gardening.

Carolyn Jenson,
Sod-Top Gardener

Carolyn Jenson describes herself unhesitatingly as a disciple of Bernard McLaughlin. "He inspired me to garden on a grand scale," she said. She visited him often and they became fast friends. Many of the plants in her garden originally came from his. In the ten years since this article first appeared, Carolyn and David Jenson have expanded their gardens and welcomed a thousand visitors every summer. (To find information on their flourishing nursery, florist, and wedding design business, as well as directions to the garden, see Appendix.) Bear Ridge Bower, with its "zillions" of flowers, offers a third example of a successful cottage garden (along with those of Bing Etzel and Nellie Davis) in the chilly hills of Franklin County.

Using a unique method they call "sod-top gardening," and endless hours of inspired labor, Carolyn and David Jenson have transformed an old, overgrown hilltop farm in western Maine into a breathtaking oasis of color in the wilderness. Surprisingly, all the well-loved perennials one usually expects to find in Maine's gentler coastal climate—delphiniums, roses, lilies, peonies, foxgloves, irises, herbs— also flourish here in the harsh weather of the state's rugged western mountains. The Jensons' twenty-acre domain straddles the border between Strong and New Vineyard. They have aptly christened it "Bear Ridge Bower."

Bower it certainly is. On either side of the drive that dead-ends at the Jensons' gray-shingled cottage, free-form "island" gardens— one even shaped like a heart—spill their flowery burden over lichen-covered rock borders. To the left they surround each of seven old Baldwin apple trees. Beyond these, in a sunny clearing, a spectacular perennial border rises from a low hedge of chartreuse lady's mantle and furry gray lamb's ears across ascending rows of old garden favorites to a backdrop of eight-foot delphiniums. Their myriad shades of blue and lavender are set off by rosy foxgloves and fluffy pink Queen-of-the-Prairie (*Filipendula rubra*). To the right of the drive, astilbes, ferns, bleeding heart, and hostas thrive in the dappled shade of birches and aspens carefully groomed to frame a view of the New Vineyard Mountains across the valley to the northeast. The festival of color begins in early spring with bulbs naturalized throughout the garden, and continues un-abated well into October with late-blooming asters and chrysanthemums.

As for the bears of Bear Ridge, they are quite real. Along with the deer, they visit nearby wild apple trees and a seventy-five-year-old blackberry patch, legacies of the nineteenth-century farm that Carolyn Jenson's father purchased in the early 1950s. The farmhouse, beyond repair, was demolished, and the family vacationed at a hunting camp they built in a field on the other side of the ridge, where it looks northwestward to the Saddle-back range. Carolyn and David returned to the mountaintop ten years ago to find respite from big-city life in Seattle, and lived in the cabin for four years while David built their "Shaker-Danish Cape," an eclectic tribute to the first old farmhouse and the simple lifestyle it represented.

The site they chose was originally the orchard, but the ancient Baldwins, once the source of a substantial crop exported to England, were lost in a forest of fifty-year-old ash and poplar. When most of the trees were cut to liberate the apples and a few other desirable specimens, Carolyn was confronted with a forest of stumps, up to twelve inches across and often only a foot apart. And thus, indirectly, was born "sod-top gardening."

"I couldn't help David build the house, so I got busy doing gardens," Carolyn explains. "I also couldn't dig the stumps out, so I got the bright idea of laying wet newspaper on the ground and covering it with spoiled hay and horse dressing." Although she was familiar with the use of newspaper and hay mulch for garden paths, Carolyn had never seen anyone use them to create a garden in the woods. The stumps were cut as close to the ground as possible. Wetting the newspapers helped to mold them over the stumps and roots. Horse dressing and thirty bales of spoiled hay were added to make raised beds six inches deep. When Carolyn sets out a plant, she clears a space at least twelve inches in diameter and fills it with good loam to provide the proper nutrient balance. It takes a couple of years for the horse dressing to decompose and become incorporated with the topsoil, but plants thrive in the rich growing medium.

"We were really encouraged about this method after a soil scientist came on a garden tour last year," Carolyn says. "He was absolutely amazed. He dug around to see what three-year-old sod-top garden soil looked like. He found a complete breakdown of the dressing, excellent granulation, lots of worm

KEVIN SHIELDS

Rosy Asiatic lilies adorn native white birch in Carolyn Jenson's carefully maintained garden.

castings, good oxygenation, beautiful soil texture. He called the method revolutionary." The expert also pointed out that the stumps and perennial weeds in the sod, decaying as they were deprived of light, would supply food for soil organisms for as long as a decade.

Carolyn applies everything she has learned from courses in soil science, botany, and landscaping at Southern Maine Technical College, the garden books she collects and reads avidly, and the many other gardeners with whom she shares information. Every fall she mows down all the spent perennial stalks, composts them, and faithfully applies lime, along with another inch or two of mulch, to all her gardens. During the summer she supplements the soil with 10-10-10 or Miracle-Gro to make up for the high nitrogen depletion that results from the composting sawdust in the horse dressing.

The results of all this thoughtful care and hard work are fabulous. Carolyn has found that thanks to the excellence of the soil, even plants for which full sunlight is recommended do remarkably well in the island beds surrounding the apple trees and the woodland gardens she is constantly carving out of the underbrush. David has carefully pruned the

venerable Baldwin trees to reveal the gnarled sculpture of their trunks and thick branches. "He calls them his 'megabonsai,'" Carolyn says. The apple trees were sick and spindly, starved for sunlight and strangled by the second-growth forest. Now they are heavy with foliage and fruit.

A brilliant foil for the curving island beds that surround the apple trees and hundred-year-old lilacs is the straight, 150-foot-long English border. Thrift dictated that this area, now open and sunny, was the only section that could be cleared of stumps, cultivated, and "farmed" in the traditional manner: row upon row of season-long blossom, and a rich variety

KEVIN SHIELDS

The Jensons reclaimed an old, overgrown orchard to build their hybrid
"Shaker-Danish Cape" and lush gardens on a western Maine hilltop.

The Grand Masters of Maine Gardening

of vegetables and berries in their plots beyond the flowers. All flourish under the same regimen of compost, horse dressing, and the green-thumb intuition that Carolyn lavishes on their neighbors in the sod-top beds.

Carolyn's delphiniums, at least a hundred magnificent specimens in every shade of blue and lavender, live up to the name 'Pacific Giants'. "This soil is incredibly adapted to delphiniums," she says. "They love a sweet pH, a neutral soil." She discovered this when she planted them accidentally in an area where brush piles had been burned. The alkaline wood ashes produced amazing results. The plants are sometimes three feet in diameter, with sturdy stems that seldom need staking. Carolyn has a bag of tricks that provides extra delphinium insurance. When the plants are small she places a cage made of green wire fencing around each one. The plants grow up in and around the eighteen-inch-high cages. When heavy wind and rain threaten the full-grown plants, she ties green hemp twine loosely around the entire plant. It disappears among the foliage. "If I know it's going to blow and rain when they're in full bloom," she adds, "I pull the [stalks] together like a teepee and tie [them]. Then I go out in the morning and shake it to get the weight of the water out of the blossoms and untie it. You *can* save delphiniums from breaking."

An inveterate seed saver and utilizer of volunteer plants that spring up in her fertile soil, Carolyn was not deterred by the traditional wisdom that delphiniums don't come true from seed. She defied convention and scattered seed from one of her best specimens. "Thousands of delphiniums came up," she says. "They're absolutely beautiful plants, every color. I took about three hundred to our garden club sale."

When the Jensons first came to the mountain, they were primarily in search of quiet isolation, but their lives have taken a new turn recently. For several years they kept a very low profile while Carolyn poured her energy into creating a garden and David built the house. David's building skills are a spin-off of his craft as a piano technician and restorer. Carolyn, a trained nurse by profession, recalls working forty-eight-hour hospital shifts to pay for building materials, renewing her strength and spirit with several days of gardening in between.

"We were quiet, glad just to live here. Nobody knew we were here—we thought," Carolyn muses. But they were wrong. Two women whom she had met through the Mt. Blue Area Garden Club, the only organization she had joined, were quietly keeping an eye on them. "Mary Davis and Mildred Morrison, whose Uncle Fredericks built this farm, would come up in their Jeep, two little old ladies in their eighties, just to see what was happening," she recalls with amusement. "It was four years before we ever knew they were watching us. One day Mary asked if the garden club could come here for their spring pilgrimage. And that was the first garden party here." The garden parties and tours continue.

As the Jensons have gradually come out of seclusion, Carolyn, who long since gave up nursing, finds herself ready to become a businesswoman on a more public scale. For some time she has been quietly framing pressed flowers and combining them with calligraphy in "Maine Cottage Garden Creations." For several years she has also been raising artemisia for the dried flower market. Recently she landed a major contract to supply it to L.L. Bean for their new line of flower arrangements.

Meanwhile, her burgeoning blossoms have become so prolific that she has begun to provide flowers for area weddings. "You can pick and pick all day and not even notice it," she says. She recalls with delight one summer morning at five o'clock "while the dew was still on the roses. We walked around in our bare feet and picked buckets of irises, lupines, peonies, heliotrope for fragrance, caraway in bloom for white." One wedding, Carolyn's brother's, actually took place in the garden last fall. The setting was so beautiful that she's now thinking of catering weddings and creating a series of floral settings to be in full bloom at every turn of the season as a backdrop for wedding photos.

Carolyn's endless supply of seedlings has inspired a nursery business as well. For years she has been giving away plants and has only begun to listen to all the people who insist on paying for them. "This dignifies what you're doing," they've told her. "I've never thought of it that way, but it's also an expression of giving back to the giver," she reasons. "So many times people who come

"So many times the people who come here to visit the gardens want to do something in return."

here to visit the gardens want to do something in return. So I'm starting to put into play right here the nursing attitude of service and contribution to humanity. And I'm also learning something about free enterprise." Community service is still a high priority for Carolyn, who has become chairman of the garden club's beautification committee, in charge of maintaining the many public gardens in Farmington.

Carolyn Jenson is convinced that encouraging people to enjoy flowers, gardens, and gardening itself is an important mission. "It's sort of a wellness therapy for me," she says. "I've been able to be well just by being here and inspiring other people to pursue it. A lot of other people, dozens and dozens of gardeners, have inspired me. It's become a lifestyle for me, all based on God's natural world. I think it's a human instinct to love nature and gardens, and to learn about them. It's a deprivation not to have that as part of our lives."

Wild Asters,
Beautiful and Bountiful

Wild asters gracing the fall fields remind us that the original gardener from whom we take example is Mother Nature herself. No need to update this timeless horticulturist. But sadly, the wildflower expert, Scott O'Connor, and his nursery, are no longer with us.

Asters. The last fling of wildflower color before all goes gray and brown. Some come with the goldenrod in late August, as evocative an envoy of the turning season as the first crocus that hails the coming of spring. By mid-September, the purples, lavenders, and pinks of wild asters have woven a royal carpet at the feet of the crowned heads of maple and beech blazing at the meadow's edge and along the roadsides. The goldenrod fades to gray-feathered stalks but still the asters persist, a patch of deep purple here, a puff of palest lilac there, lingering reminders of the riches of the season just past.

At close range, asters—with their yellow-to-burgundy centers from which radiate long lavender, purple, white, rose, or pale blue petals—look much like daisies, their cousins in the composite family, which filled the wildflower meadows with the same generous abandon earlier in the season.

To some, the annual beneficence of asters is sufficient unto itself. Why ask more of these simple flowers than just that they be there to make summer's final, wistful farewell? Others, yearning perhaps to grasp their fleeting essence, want to know more—and there is a lot more to know. More than five hundred varieties of asters are found around the globe. Peterson's *A Field Guide to Wildflowers* and Marilyn Dwelley's *Summer & Fall Wildflowers*

of New England can help identify the more common ones in our area, but even experienced botanists have difficulty distinguishing among the endless crosses that occur in the wild and at the hands of hybridizers eager to capture and improve upon so much beauty.

Asters are plentiful, not endangered, and easy to transplant into the home garden.

RAND RAABE

Telling species of wild asters apart is no simple matter, but all blossom prolifically and last for days as cut flowers.

Asters are easily domesticated, bringing dependable, welcome color at a time when most plants are fast fading away.

Gathered by the roadside or cut in the dooryard, they will also grace with a kind of Shaker simplicity any flower arrangement, whether in an old milk can or a Meissen vase. Fortunately for us, the greatest assortment of the world's asters flourishes in North America, the types varying from the Northeast to the Rockies to the West Coast. In Maine, the four- to eight-foot-tall New England asters (*Aster novae angliae*) whose rich, pure purple floods acres of roadside fields, and the other, paler asters whose smoky lavenders frost the hillsides, are the most familiar members of the tribe. The "frosties" are most probably a combination of the smaller-flowered Lowrie's and the heart-leaved, or blue wood aster, according to Scott O'Connor of North Temperate Wildflowers, in Jefferson. But there are at least a dozen more varieties that thrive from the coast to the western mountains and to the farmlands and wildernesses of Aroostook County. Serious amateur botanists can look for the heart-shaped leaves of some and the more linear leaves of others when trying to make identifications. Either type can range in color from white to every shade of pink, blue, and violet.

The four- to eight-inch heart-shaped foliage of the large-leaved aster carpets dry woods and is often used as a ground cover by woodland gardeners. Several varieties of taller white wood asters brighten open trails and abandoned clearings from June or July through October. Even earlier is an aster look-alike, the daisy fleabane, which can appear as early as May and is distinguished from true asters by its myriad fine, silky petals.

The New England aster and the willow-leaved aster prefer moister situations, but most asters thrive in the dry, light soils of roadsides, upland fields, and open woodlands, a boon to gardeners with difficult soil conditions. The alpine aster, whose soft purple flowers rise on short stems above a tight rosette of leaves, is found on New England mountaintops and has been propagated as a charming addition to the rock garden. Another valuable aster for the wildflower gardener is fairly common but not terribly showy in the wild, where it is often found on roadsides and along railroad tracks. It's the stiff aster, a small, compact bush. Its fine, needle-like leaves of a deep glossy green and its little blue flowers call to mind the herb rosemary.

Most attractive of our native asters in many respects is the New York aster (*Aster novae-belgii*), more common along the coast and, along with the New England aster, the source of all that late-summer purple. Shorter than the New England aster, with larger, tighter lavender blossoms and more spreading flower heads, *novae-belgii* is undoubtedly the progenitor of the many varieties of Michaelmas daisy cultivated for years here and in Europe (so-called because they bloom around St. Michael's Day, September 29). Although the New York aster succeeds in Maine, it is less plentiful than the New England aster, perhaps because it has been uprooted from the wild so often and transplanted into gardens.

It's no wonder that wild perennial asters, with their irresistible appeal to the eye and their uncanny enchantment to the heart, have been collected and cultivated for generations. Experienced gardeners have learned that because asters blossom so late—and so pro-lifically—they can extend the showiness of a perennial border by weeks. A few wild asters and more of their cultivated cousins are available from seed catalogs, but they are easy to propagate from the wild. Clumps can be dug and transplanted virtually at any time during the growing season. Asters can also be grown from cuttings, but they're just as easy to raise from seed. Be sure the seeds are totally ripe—dark brown in color, advises Scott O'Connor, who raises hundreds of asters. The seeds can be separated from their dandelion-like "parachutes" by storing them in a paper bag and shaking it occasionally. The tiny brown seeds will collect in the bottom of the bag. Sow them indoors in flats in early spring, sparsely to prevent crowding and damping off. Once flourishing in the garden, asters can be pruned regularly to encourage heavier bloom.

Fortunately for us, the greatest assortment of the world's asters flourishes in North America.

Captive in the garden or running wild over the countryside, asters never fail to touch an elusive chord of nostalgia, especially if they're discovered in faraway places. Author Peter Matthiessen, in *The Snow Leopard*, wrote of finding them along a mountain path while trekking in Nepal in the Himalayas one October, "pale lavender asters much like those that would be abundant now in woods and fields at home."

Asters, harvest time, home. Who hasn't felt the same stirring "at the deep heart's core" when rounding a bend in the road and coming upon a cloud of lavender asters?

Corinne Mann's Daylilies

Most Maine gardeners grow at least a small assortment of well-loved garden flowers, but there are some who devote their major efforts to a single species. Corinne Mann can rightfully be called a "Dean of Maine Daylilies," having become an authority on their culture and history in the forty-year process of creating a still-evolving collection of nearly a hundred varieties. My phone call to find out what she has been doing since our original interview in 1983 caught Corinne as she was off to teach a class in ikebana, her second love. Now in her eighties and going it alone since her husband's passing, she planted bulbs last fall and has embarked on a new project—growing cranesbill geraniums of every color. "I don't feel old," she says with undiminished enthusiasm. She is still advising garden clubs, chairing workshops, and "lovin' life."

Corinne Mann stands foursquare on her primary gardening principle: "I only grow what will do well for me." Fortunately for her, and for many people who drive by her early-nineteenth-century home in Kittery Point to catch a glimpse of midsummer glory, or who stop in for a closer look at the magnificent specimens in her garden, daylilies (and a lot of other things) do exceedingly well for her.

Nearly a hundred not-so-common varieties of this common old-fashioned flower flourish along the stone walls and rocky ledges that rise from the sloping lawn to her front door. Pinks, golds, creams, delicate apricots, and vibrant oranges, with here and there a splash of crimson, stand vividly against a background of dark brown clapboards and weathered shingles. It's a tapestry that has been more than thirty years in the weaving, but Corinne doesn't hesitate to tear out a section of the woof and start the pattern over if she's not pleased or if she gets a new inspiration. "If I don't like something where it is, I take it up

and replant it, live or die. It's a renewable resource," she declares with good humor.

Gardening is not an acquired taste for Corinne Mann but a heritage that "just came naturally" to her. A home garden was a big part of her childhood in Raymond, a few miles north of Portland. "My father loved gardening—vegetables, flowers. He'd often come into the house with some new flower in his hand to show us," she recalls. "In spring I was always out before the snow was off the ground, hunting wildflowers." Her early enthusiasm for wildflowers has never waned, as an extensive collection of native plants bordering the marsh behind her home attests. Wildflowers as well as daylilies are among the subjects of her frequent illustrated lectures to garden clubs and other groups.

Corinne and her husband, Daniel, moved to Kittery from Raymond when he changed jobs from the S. D. Warren paper mill in Westbrook to the Portsmouth Naval Shipyard. At first they lived in an apartment, where she raised beans, carrots, and chrysanthemums in a three- by six-foot garden in front of the windows. Then they went house hunting, and the day in 1948 that they found their present home she started planning the first stone wall. The following spring the couple spaded up an old vegetable garden on the front lawn, and Corinne took all kinds of annual seeds, threw them in a paper bag, shook them up, and scattered them over the ground. "I just have to have something growing," she says.

"The only things here when we came were a Seckel pear at the front corner, three peonies down the main walk, and an old asparagus bed," she continues. "We dug up the asparagus, and the roots were the size of bushel baskets. I didn't want the walk there, so I got rid of it. The pear tree is still here. Everything else, we've planted." This includes a huge white birch more than thirty years old, clumps of venerable arborvitae, and a twenty-

five-foot Dawn redwood, now about twenty years old, that started out as a four-inch potted seedling. Behind Corinne's modest and straightforward manner lies innate artistic vision. She has placed the trees advantageously to interrupt the long line of the house's facade and built her stone walls along the horizontal flow of the ledge, effactually tying the tall, Federal-style building to its surroundings. Dan started the corner of the first stone wall, but all the rest of the walls and gardens are the work of Corinne's own hands.

Daylilies didn't take over Corinne's life at Kittery Point immediately. She started with tall delphiniums, but they couldn't take the storms and strong sea winds blowing across Pepperell Cove from the open Atlantic beyond. Next she tried floribunda and tea roses, but two hurricanes did away with that project. Always a garden club member (she belongs to

Although each blossom lasts only a day, so many blooms are produced on each plant that Corinne Mann's midsummer show of daylilies lasts for several weeks.

the Harborside Garden Club of Kittery and New Castle, New Hampshire, and is past president of the Garden Club Federation of Maine), Corinne fell in love with daylilies at a club conference in Orono. Betty Hayward, of West Scarborough, showed a slide of *Hemerocallis* 'Canary' that took her breath away. She got herself a root of it and was off.

Soon she discovered that her soil and location were ideal for this hardy herbaceous perennial, and her collection grew until now she has about a hundred varieties, each clump tagged with a neat botanical marker. These are mostly for the benefit of the dozens of individuals and groups that visit her garden between July 10 and August 1 every year when it is officially open to the public. For her own part, she needs no markers. She knows every one of her daylilies by heart.

Corinne's love affair with daylilies paralleled the development of the genus as an important component of American gardens. "Thirty years ago, the daylily was practically unknown except for the tawny wayside lily (*Hemerocallis fulva*) and the early-blooming lemon lily (*H. flava*)," she explains. Occasionally she consults her little black "lecture book," the veteran of many years of gardening talks, as she recounts the botanical saga. "Also known as the homestead or privy lily, *H. fulva* was carried across the country by women moving west," she continues. The lemon lily was known to the Romans and Egyptians. Daylilies are a plant long cultivated in eastern Europe. They originally grew in the woodland margins of the plains of northern China. They were introduced into Europe and America by various routes as they were discovered, some as late as the mid-nineteenth century. By 1890 most of the ten or so known species of *Hemerocallis* had arrived in North America. Corinne has them all in her garden. Last summer she

established them in a special new spot of their own to distinguish them from the masses of hybrids that dominate her collection. The corner is marked off by a pool in the rocks and a backdrop of ancient *Cotoneaster divaricatus*, whose thick, well-pruned branches form a decorative grille brightened by scarlet berries in the fall. (When garden flowers have bloomed their last, robins and cedar waxwings enjoying a late-season berry feast prolong the color.)

The first hybrid daylily, Corinne notes, was an apricot-colored variety produced by British botanist George Yeld in 1892, a cross between *H. middendorfii* and *H. flava*. Since then more than thirty thousand varieties have been developed, mostly in the last thirty years. Choosing a mere hundred from among them has been a sometimes perplexing but always engaging task. "Most people's favorite flower is the rose, but not mine," she says matter-of-factly, but a tender note creeps into her voice as she describes her favorite. "Daylilies are . . . so many things. The colors, the forms, the shapes, the textures are so varied: crepe, satin finish, diamond-dusted, star, wheel, ruffled, recurved, spider . . ."

The ideal daylily characteristics, cited by this card-carrying member of the American Hemerocallis Society and former show judge, include "a scape [stem] with a gentle arch, which sways in the breeze, not a stiff one that can be broken. It should not sweep the ground or fall into the mud." She has a feeling, bred of years of daylily culture, that the older varieties and diploid hybrids have a better growth and survival record than the fancier new tetraploids. Aesthetically she prefers the "loose gracefulness" of the less highly bred varieties to the thickened stems and huge blossoms now being developed.

Color is another matter—the more unusual the better. Starting with the original oranges and yellows, daylily breeders have developed pinks, greens, reds, and lavenders, along with seemingly infinite variations on apricot, melon, and peach. The long-sought Holy Grail of hybridizers is a pure white, as yet approached only in the ivories and creams. Corinne's white daylily is 'Shepherd's Light', a delicate ivory, but her preference leans toward the pink, as her all-time favorites suggest. "If I could have only three daylilies," she states without hesitation, "they'd be 'Kuan Yin', a rose with a green throat, because it always looks so beautifully crisp and tailored; 'Pink Limeade', which has just the faintest glow, a pink haze that makes me think of lemonade (I've filled a big part of my garden with it.); and 'Moon Dancer,' with its crepe-like texture and soft golden yellow." A ruffled golden called 'Heirloom Lace' she recommends for its greater tolerance for shade, one of the few daylilies she grows in her back garden among the trees. The reds she finds less appealing, but one that takes her fancy is a scarlet called 'Grandfather Time'.

Corinne Mann's secret of gardening success is as instinctive as her love of flowers. Like a prize-winning cook, she depends on the look and feel of her work in progress. Rather than any standardized recipe or formula, her rule of thumb is the pragmatic "what happens here." She has never had her soil tested, yet she hasn't had to add quantities of either lime or acidifiers. Daylilies like a soil that's neutral to a bit acid, she says. She feels fortunate to have land where things grow "with the help of a fertilizer once in a while." If she's setting out a plant that has arrived in a pot, she digs a hole and "puddles in" a little Hy-trous (a brand of liquid fertilizer), puts in the plant, and adds a little more Hy-trous on top of the ground. She uses the same liquid fertilizer in a hose nozzle attachment designed for fine-spray fo-

Yellow daylilies are all-time favorites.

liage feeding, "if I think they need it." Although she doesn't claim to be an organic gardener, Corinne makes use of every bit of discarded vegetation, even small branches, which she puts through a mechanical shredder. She keeps it in a pile for mulch, spreading it where the soil "looks poorly on top." How does she tell? "It has a look that all the goodness is out of it" is the closest she comes to a scientific explanation.

Daylilies do best in full sun, says Corinne, though a few hours a day of dappled shade in midsummer does not deter their blooming. She has plenty of open, sunny lawn where she can expand whenever she wishes. To start a new bed from scratch, she removes the sod and spades in an ample amount of organic material. For a bed six by eighteen feet, she mixes together "about a coffee can of each" of Bovung (commercial cow manure), pure potash, and superphosphate, and works the mixture well into the soil. "Every spring I add more potash and phosphate, the two things that leach out of our soil fastest. They're needed for color, both for bloom and foliage, and for strong stems." When daylilies are set out, she notes, the crown, where the roots join

BRIAN VANDEN BRINK

the leaves, should be no more than an inch and a half to two inches below the soil surface. Otherwise, the plant will not bloom. She sticks chiefly to midseason daylilies, having learned that garden catalog promises of successive bloom, from "extra early" to "very late," are not necessarily kept by daylilies themselves. They bloom when they're ready, mostly in midsummer.

The only pests that give Corinne's daylilies much trouble are earwigs and slugs. Earwigs like to lurk in the blossoms before demolishing them. "I cup my hand around a bloom, blow into it, and when they drop out, I stomp them. I've even gotten so I can pinch

them," she says with devilish satisfaction. On slugs, she has tried beer and rings of ashes without much luck. So far, the method that has worked best for her is the early morning ritual with a jar of hot, salted water and a spoon, scooping up the slugs and drowning them. Avoiding heavy mulches and cleaning up dead foliage where slugs camp out is important, she adds. Weeds she controls by early spring hoeing. "If you want to eliminate witchgrass, you have to start pulling it in April," she advises. "Otherwise, forget it." The shade canopy and thick growth habits of daylilies are also good weed deterrents.

Daylilies are persistent survivors in Maine. Some of Corinne's have been in the same spot for twenty-five years. On the whole, they don't seem to mind crowding, she observes. But if her keen eye spots clumps that show signs of thinning out, if the blooms look smaller, if the spikes are not so full, it's time to separate them. She digs out the whole clump and pries it apart gently, using two spading forks placed back to back. If the clump defies division, she may "take it by the hair of the head, drag it down to the backyard, and set it on the ground, where it will probably thrive." Most varieties grow well in any climate and are not too particular about soil. True evergreen types are not hardy enough for the North, and the very hardy ones, which need a cold winter dormant period, do not do well in the Deep South, she says.

Corinne's garden tapestry takes on new shape, color, and texture by several means. The annual Hemerocallis Show in Worcester, Massachusetts, about mid-July, offers a dazzling display of new cultivars to tempt the daylily fancier. Regular reading of horticultural publications—particularly the *Daylily Journal*, published by the American Hemerocallis Society—and growers' catalogs whets her appetite. By midwinter, she succumbs to the

Corrine Mann enjoys her garden from inside or outside her bay window, with its view of Pepperell Cove.

BRIAN VANDEN BRINK

The Grand Masters of Maine Gardening

perennial gardener's itch and sends in an order to her favorite supplier, Gilbert H. Wild and Son, Inc. (Sarcoxie, Missouri 64862), whose plants are "the cleanest and nicest of any."

Known as the "poor man's orchid," daylilies can range in price from $1.50 to $250. Corinne watches the prices of the newly named cultivars as they decline year by year after their introduction. When one she especially covets reaches a reasonable level, she will purchase it. Space for her new acquisitions is made by extending the garden and selling off quantities of extras when she divides old clumps. In placing plants, she again relies on her unfailing intuition. "I don't have any special color plan. They blend so beautifully that you don't have to be careful. This year I'm concentrating on filling empty spaces. You can enjoy established plants while you wait for the new ones to come into bloom. Some take three to five years."

Though daylilies far outnumber every other resident of her garden, Corinne doesn't raise them exclusively. A little sheltered terrace under the kitchen bay window teems with chives, rue, and lamb's ears. Thymes grow in her flagstone walks, and Greek marjoram flourishes down back. A few annuals—marigolds for color, alyssum and nicotiana for fragrance—and favorite perennials such as poppies and peonies also find their places. In spring, orange Emperor tulips and blue grape hyacinths, scilla, and forget-me-nots parade in front of the sun-warmed stone walls.

Recently Corinne's daylilies have encountered rivals for her affections in Siberian and Japanese iris and hosta. "The iris are like daylilies. Each bloom lasts only one day, but they keep coming and coming," she says. One of her particular loves is a little Siberian called 'Flight of Butterflies', which looks just like its name when a breeze blows across it. She's developing a hosta garden in the pines under the back kitchen window and already has collected twenty-two varieties. True lilies are also finding their way into selected nooks.

When one considers the essential simplicity of Corinne Mann's gardening—concentrating on a few carefully chosen and relatively undemanding species, making use of rock and tree formations—and the spare, Shaker-influenced interior decor of the home that she and Dan have restored, her other enthusiasms, including classical Japanese flower arranging and landscape design, are entirely in character. A member of the Kittery Point Chapter of the Ikenobo Ikebana Society, she exhibited a traditional Japanese arrangement at the International Design Society Festival of Flowers at the Cathedral of St. John the Divine in New York City last fall. As president of the state Garden Club Federation, she was instrumental in organizing an eight-year series of landscape courses in Maine under the auspices of the national organization. She holds a landscape design critic's certificate, has advised town planning boards, and has taught landscape design. She was a charter member of Governor John H. Reed's Keep Maine Scenic committee, served as secretary to the state Critical Areas Committee under Governor Kenneth M. Curtis, and has done historical plant research for Strawbery Banke in nearby Portsmouth, New Hampshire.

Such activities in the line of duty and pleasure are largely in the past for this energetic, silver-haired lady, but only because so many new avenues remain to be explored. Ikebana, irises, and hostas are among them, but her first love is still the magnificent collection of daylilies in her front yard. "I recommend that all gardeners have at least one clump [of daylilies]," she says with a smile, "even if they have to fight the slugs and earwigs for them. There's just nothing like them."

Five Hundred Enchanting Irises

Bernard McLaughlin helped Joan and Russell Moors start the garden in their Auburn backyard more than forty-five years ago, and they remained close friends until McLaughlin died. "We miss him very much," Joan said recently. "Some of his plants are still growing in our garden." With a master like McLaughlin to guide them, it is no wonder that by the time this article was originally published, in 1986, they had become experts in the field of their choice, tall bearded irises. The irises still thrive, along with their growing collections of hostas and daylilies. Joan and Russell are still active in the Maine Iris Society, as well as the Maine Hosta Society.

What's in a name? An iris by any other name might ravish the eye alone, but call it 'Grand Waltz', and its lavender ball-gown ruffles seem to dance on the June breeze to the strains of Strauss. Name another blossom 'Latin Lover', and its sunset hues take on a more romantic glow. The deep purple and olive-yellow tones of 'Shaman' conjure dark magic. 'Wild Berry,' a luscious black-raspberry sherbet, and 'Hoca Mocha', a yummy parfait, really do look good enough to eat.

But even if you don't stop to read the labels, every sense quickens as you stroll through the mid-June garden of Joan and Russell Moors. Row on row of vibrant bloom remind you that the family name is Iris, from the Greek for rainbow. Hundreds of visitors have shared the breathtaking experience and have gone home to try to capture some of the same beauty in their own gardens.

"We really want people to start growing irises," says Joan (pronounced Jo-Ann). "It's one reason we have the open house every year."

The Moorses themselves were inspired nearly thirty years ago by the magnificent near-by gardens of Everett Greaton and Brooks Quimby, founders of the Maine Iris Society. They joined the society soon after its formation and have been among the state's most active iris enthusiasts ever since. "We were intrigued by the tremendous variation in color," says Russ. "Irises come in almost any color in the rainbow but pure black. We've found that the real fun is adding new varieties we've never grown, at the same time keeping the best of the old. Some gardeners always go for the very new and discard older ones quickly. We have the tendency to be more conservative. That's why you see two or three names in Joan's collection that are extremely old. They may be color patterns that can't be duplicated in today's iris."

The Moorses insist, however, that they don't necessarily prefer irises to other flowers. The backyard of their home on Auburn's Park Avenue—not the grand boulevard it sounds like, but a suburban road on the edge of town—is one huge perennial garden. Of their thirty-eight four-foot-wide beds—roughly nine hundred running feet in all—nearly half are devoted to swaths of glorious irises. Most of the five hundred varieties they grow are tall bearded irises, but there are dwarf, median, Siberian, and Japanese types as well. "We enjoy them a great deal once a year, but we wouldn't have only irises. We truly enjoy a perennial garden and all the different types available," says Russ. "One thing a person has to realize with a perennial garden is that he will never have a mass of color except at unusual times—like when the iris are in bloom. Otherwise, it's just a spot here and there."

Joan adds that their perennials are a collection rather than a study in mass plantings, "a taste of everything." They are constantly in search of new perennials to try, even making a special trip to Massachusetts every year to add to the mix. Old plants are often relegated to the storage garden at the rear of the grounds to make way for new specimens.

"But the primary thing with us is the iris," she continues, "and then the daylilies. We have about 125 varieties coming right after the iris. That's our color for the summer. After that, tall phlox will be our mainstay."

Siberian and Japanese irises, which require more moisture, and median irises, which Joan says don't look good mixed in with the tall bearded ones, bloom among the succession of other perennials. But the extensive beds devoted exclusively to tall bearded iris at the front of the garden revert to plain green when the last bloom fades at the end of June. That doesn't mean they can be forgotten, however. Caring for five hundred irises that in a good year produce approximately two thousand bloom stalks is a year-round proposition. The most irksome physical job is the constant weeding they require; the most mentally exhausting one is the extensive record-keeping that goes into charting their progress and planning for the coming season.

"Weeds are the biggest chore," Joan says. "If I do a bed or two a day, five days a week,

BENJAMIN MAGRO

Tall bearded irises display as many hues as a summer sunset.

by the time I get done, it's time to start again. The hardest are the irises. All you're doing around iris is just breaking off the witchgrass, so it's up again right away. I'd rather do ten perennial beds than one of iris." The Moorses are even considering herbicides, but only as a last resort. One step they have taken is to stop adding more iris beds and to extend their daylily collection instead. "Daylilies are a

Although Joan states that "you have to realize that you can't grow everything," she and Russell grow about five hundred varieties of irises at any given time, and they are continually testing new ones.

hundred percent easier to care for than irises," Joan asserts.

The Moorses divide the labors of gardening and share the satisfactions. Joan, who has more time at home, copes with the tedium of constant maintenance. In his free time, Russ tackles the heavier work of dividing overgrown clumps and edging and rebuilding beds, with some help from their twenty-year-old son, who, with his sister, does most of the mowing. Russ recently returned to the shoe industry as a purchasing agent for Eastland Shoe in Freeport after a brief hiatus from a lifetime in busi-

ness. He took another job temporarily rather than accept a position overseas that would have meant leaving his garden. Joan is a tax preparer for H & R Block from January 1 to April 15, an ideal work schedule for a gardener. Two of their four grown children live at home; the other two live out of state.

Experimenting with new varieties is the name of the game for iris growers. The Moorses add as many as thirty specimens each year. "We don't usually add more than one or two new introductions [plants offered by hybridizers for the first time] a year," says Joan. "It's too expensive, and I don't think it's as much fun as adding things that we've learned from reading are really good." New varieties are planted in a special circle around the rose bed at the center of the garden, where they can be watched closely.

"We can be very harsh with new varieties. Some never make it," says Russ. "If an iris doesn't perform well, we get rid of it. If it does well for a couple of years, I take a whole clump, with a big ball of earth, and move it into the display garden. It doesn't even know it's been moved."

One of the difficulties with experimentation in Maine, he points out, is that many varieties of iris hybridized on the West Coast are not compatible with the New England climate. Some simply winterkill. Others may grow for years but never bloom. "Actually, Maine is not a bad iris climate as long as you get varieties that do well," says Joan. "Some of the award-winning irises rated highest by the American Iris Society we can't do anything with. At first it's frustrating. Then you have to realize you can't grow everything, so we just don't grow them."

With five hundred varieties of irises flourishing, the Moorses obviously have mastered the method for growing those which do thrive

The Grand Masters of Maine Gardening

in Maine's trying weather. A primary requirement for tall bearded iris is good drainage. All the Moorses' perennial beds are raised, and last summer they undertook the major task of rebuilding several that had subsided to ground level, where the iris were doing poorly. Their yard's slightly alkaline, sandy soil with its natural underlayment of gravel is ideal for irises, which need a certain amount of moisture in dry weather but develop rot very easily if the ground remains sodden.

System is everything when keeping track of a garden this size. Every plant is labeled, but Joan can identify them without that aid. "It's like having five hundred children out there, all with names," she says. She is the official custodian of the garden notebook, which lists every plant that is in the garden. Each bed has its own number and a map of its layout. If a label is lost to the lawnmower, or Joan's prodigious memory fails, the plant can still be identified. "We have a joke here in the house that if we ever have a fire, the only thing you need to worry about, other than yourself and the dog, is the garden notebook," says Joan.

The notebook records everything that goes into the garden and everything that comes out. What comes out—especially in the iris department, where room is constantly in demand for new additions—depends on a methodical evaluation system Russ developed. Every iris plant is reviewed annually and given a rating of one to five on a checklist. "If it gets a one, it's about ready to go out," he explains. "If it gets a five, it's in good standing. In between, it could go either way. After two or three years, you pretty much weed out the ones you're going to get

rid of by looking at their history. One year it may get a low rating for winter damage or something else you can't control. If the same plant gets a low rating for several years, the reasons may vary: quality of bloom, lack of bloom, lack of growth. In general, it's not compatible for some reason." Even when it's on the way out, a plant is often transferred to the storage garden for a second chance before the final decision.

The qualities growers look for in iris, besides hardiness and good growth, include color, form, bud count, and branching. The last two are especially important for prolonged bloom. Fashions in iris forms change as hybridizers explore new possibilities. "People don't realize how much irises have changed over the years," Joan remarks. "Take this one, for instance, 'Color Carnival'. It was hybridized in 1949. Obviously an old one, from its tailored form. The trend today is toward blockier shape, more ruffles, unusual colors. The old ones have much longer falls [the downward-hanging petals]. They don't want these 'hound dog falls' any more." "Horns" and "spoons" [fleshy extensions around the beard] are another new development. Last year a separate class for horns and spoons was added to the Maine Iris Society show to accommodate a growing number of entries of these types.

"And you haven't seen anything yet," adds Russ. "Wait five or ten years, and they'll look even more different." Hybridizers researching certain traits or specializing in a particular color sometimes come up with spectacular surprises. The Moorses so far have not taken up hybridizing, calling it too time-consuming.

The end of all this careful selection and

"Best of Show can be won by anybody, whether they raise one iris or a thousand."

Nearly half of the huge perennial garden is devoted to irises.

cultivation is the show-and-tell of iris garden-ing, the annual flower show. "As we became interested in shows," Russ relates, "we realized we had a small nucleus of active, involved people, all of them perfectionists. We tried hard to develop the Maine show as one of the finest in the eastern United States." Indeed, the Maine Iris Society's show is widely re-garded today as one of the top shows in the country. Russ maintains that that reputation developed because the show is set up in logical fashion, strictly according to American Iris Society rules; because a great deal of effort is put into the grooming and displaying of en-tries; and because accredited judges are always brought in from out of state.

The Moorses, as usual, are in the thick of the action. Russ is current president of the society, an office he also held in 1969–70. He and Joan co-chaired the show for most of its first decade and have continued to be deeply involved. In August Russ will serve for the umpteenth time as auctioneer at the society's annual sale of iris rhizomes (donated by members from their surplus), perennial plants, and garden-related items. The auction funds the iris shows and other society activities. Last year, Russ sold nearly 4,500 rhizomes in four hours, garnering almost $2,300.

"Our first real awakening to the fun of showing was when we took a Best of Show in 1966," Russ recalls. They have received the award ten times since, most recently last year, when the society established a permanent trophy for the honor to mark its twenty-fifth anniversary. The Moorses' dining room walls are almost papered with plaques recording dozens of other iris awards as well.

"Best of Show can be won by anybody, whether they raise one iris or a thousand. It just happens to be a perfect bloom on that particular day," says Russ. Both he and Joan are official judges for the American Iris Society. Entries are judged on freshness of bloom, uniformity of foliage and stems, and all-round perfection. Selecting the stalks he plans to exhibit is nearly a science in itself, as he explains: "Three or four days before the show, I take little pieces of white cotton string and drop them on stalks of iris I think are going to be good. I can watch each stalk, and if it blooms too soon, I just take the string off. You can be fooled the day before. Usually I cut the stalks then because there isn't time the morning of the show." Everything has to be ready for judging by 10 A.M. The ideal is to have a freshly opened bloom at 9:59. Iris blossoms are fragile and hard to transport. He takes them in buckets of sand. At the show, all stalks are displayed in identical containers,

plastic bleach bottles purchased some years back from a commercial supplier and stored, not surprisingly, in the Moorses' garage. Bloom stalks are grouped by color and by name within the color. If there are enough of one variety, the variety is judged separately.

Encouraging other gardeners is the aim of the Moorses and the Maine Iris Society. Preparing members to exhibit in the show is a matter of tactful education, Russ says. "We don't want to put so many conditions on entering that people won't dare to try." A few days before the show, they arrange a meeting in someone's garden, open to anyone who wants to come, Maine Iris Society member or not. Accredited judges from the society take people around in small groups, explaining what makes a good iris and pointing out the qualities they should be looking for.

"I think one of the most enjoyable activities we've had over the years is opening the garden to the public," says Russ. "It's a lot of fun to see people go through. They seldom do any damage." (He does remember one woman with an enormous pocketbook who caused him a few gray hairs. "Every time she turned a corner, the bag swung and hit a stalk.") Children are welcome as long as their parents keep an eye on them. People have come from many parts of the country and many walks of life. One local woman, an artist, spent half a summer in the garden painting. The Moorses even stored her chair in the garage.

"Meeting different people—through garden clubs, the iris societies, the parade of visitors in our backyard—has opened up a new world for us," Russ says. Both of the Moorses like to recall their own mentors and to reflect on the many people they've gotten interested in gardening. "One of the most satisfying things for any gardener," says Russ, "is to help create a new gardener."

Debbie Deal's Delphiniums

Few Maine gardens lack the July splendor of blue delphiniums, whether as a few striking stalks for highlights or as a dramatic backdrop for a colorful border. But for Debbie Deal, they became a way of life, filling a whole field overlooking Johnson Cove and Friendship Harbor. That was a dozen years ago, and it's still a delight to revisit Debbie's delphiniums en masse in the following article.

With her usual serendipity, however, she just happened to scatter a packet of mixed Japanese iris seeds in an odd corner. It was only a couple of years before the first ten plants needed to be divided, again and again. Now seven hundred huge-blossomed Japanese irises of various, unknown heritage have taken over the delphinium field, and her cut-flower business is soaring as never before. Oddly enough, Debbie had never heard of Currier McEwen.

A sadder change is that her faithful golden Lab, Jessie, has gone to dog Elysium and a bouncing young replica, Buttercup, has taken over her duties.

When icy winds howl around the gables and June is just a distant tug at the heart, it helps to imagine a sea of six-foot delphiniums—summer sky to midnight blue, lavender, pink, white, royal purple—swaying gently in a sun-warmed afternoon breeze, crowded so thickly that the aisles between their rows are impassable. But Debbie Deal wasn't thinking delphiniums as she camped out with sleeping bag, battery lantern, and portable toilet in her under-reconstruction saltwater farmhouse seven Februarys ago.

Deal didn't really have a clue—unless it was a vague idea to maybe grow a few herbs—that her escape from the nine-to-five hurly-burly of Massachusetts would lead to what has become a thriving garden business and a deeply satisfying way of life. Friendship Garden and Farm Stand on Johnson Cove, half a mile from the center of the Maine fishing village of Friendship, is well on the way to becoming as much a local institution as the classic sloops that have made the town world-famous. From miles around come seekers of fresh-picked vegetables and spectacular cut flowers, home gardeners in need of well-grown perennials, professional landscapers, and the occasional restaurant owner with a big order to fill.

"I hand out scissors, and people come in and cut their own," says Deal, a slender, exuberant woman of forty-three who has a hard time keeping up with her own boundless enthusiasms. "I charge by the size of the bouquet. It's the only way I can do it. I don't count stems. I'd be all day just doing that," she says, implying that she has a thousand other things to keep an eye on as well. People come and pick her flowers for the weddings, parties, and other events that highlight the summer season in Friendship, where the population doubles by the Fourth of July.

Customers have variety aplenty to choose

from. Delphiniums, vigorous specimens that bear as many as twenty tall spikes apiece, fill a big plot near the road for display, cutting, and drying. Their blues are set off by a nearby spread of red and yellow gaillardia. Raised beds create a brilliant patchwork—cosmos in shades of pink and red, blue bachelor buttons, larkspur, and campanulas, blazing zinnias, chartreuse lady's mantle, steeples of magenta foxgloves rising among white Shasta daisies, a rainbow of snapdragons, and a myriad of others. Among them the subtler blossoms and foliage of lavender, rosemary, thyme, and German statice add contrasting texture and the pungent fragrance of herbs. Down in the field, irises, lilies, hundreds of Canterbury bells, and a couple thousand young delphiniums are growing for sale or for next year's roadside display. By late summer, many of these delphiniums bloom in their first year, against a magnificent backdrop of trellised pink and white sweet peas. Roman-stripe rows of pale and dark green, rust, and burgundy lettuces border plots where all the usual farmstand vegetables flourish, along with the mesclun mixes that are becoming so popular, and other new varieties that have captured Deal's adventurous fancy.

"It's been an absolutely tremendous year for delphiniums, despite the fog and rain," Deal observes at the end of summer 1996. "Everything has been as lush as could be. The annual cutting garden was an enormous block of color. The lavender put on two years' growth in one season. I had pansies that were waist high."

It wasn't always like this. Looking back, she can hardly believe that when she started tilling a small patch six years ago, the soil was "like compressed driveway dirt." A landscaper friend told her to put a foot of cow manure on the whole thing. "Everybody in town said,

'You don't do that,' but it was just perfect," she recalls. "I grew a lot of lush stuff the first year. Things just went crazy. Then every year I put compost in. It's all organic. I got soil tests at first. The last two years I haven't had time for that, but things are still cranking, so I know everything is okay."

Debbie Deal's gardens overlook Friendship Harbor. Light summer fog intensifies the colors of coastal gardens and forest.

KEVIN SHIELDS

As well as the soil's fertility, Deal credits her bountiful bloom to several hives of bees she keeps for honey and for pollination. She has found that bees adore the mallow she grows in pink profusion. "Even thirty feet away, you could hear the bees in the mallow. I got almost pure mallow honey. I could see a tremendous difference after I got the bees. My neighbor even noticed it in her wildflower garden," Deal says. Though her bees were hit by the same combination of bad weather and mites that struck beekeepers throughout the state last year, they survived moderately well and have bounced back remarkably, she reports.

Deal also rejoices in a dearth of damaging pests. She tries to keep space around plants for good air circulation to discourage molds and mildews. She scrambles plantings to avoid monoculture situations that abet insect populations, and times preventative measures to interfere with insect life cycles. She takes a sash out of a barn window every spring to welcome a flock of barn swallows, which, with their tree swallow cousins nesting nearby, make a noticeable dent in the bug count. "I guess I've just been lucky," she says. She has collected reference books on insects and gardening, and calls her local extension agent for advice, but more often she relies on her accumulating experience. "In the beginning," she says, "I looked up everything, but you just start to *know* after a while." Deal now has three times the area she started with under cultivation. "That little garden where you see the asparagus was going to be my whole garden," she says, laughing. "Where I came from, their idea of gardening was putting a geranium on the doorstep. So I was overwhelmed when I came to Maine."

Deal had often visited her parents' summer cottage in Cushing before she fell prey to corporate burnout in her home state, Massachusetts. She spent a summer at her parents' cottage, looking for businesses and houses to buy. "I almost ended up buying a laundromat in Belfast," she recalls with amused horror. "At the last minute I bailed out. I knew it wasn't right for me." Her search for a house lasted six months. The woman she bought the house from, in her eighties, was leery of selling it to a "young girl" like herself. "She didn't know what a wicked worker I was," Deal says with a satisfied grin.

The house had been in the same family since 1832. When she bought it in December 1989, half the windows were missing, the kitchen wall was split a foot apart from the main house, and the well was frozen up. She set local builders to work at once. "The deal with the builders was, 'You can have the job if you let me work with you and teach me.' I picked up all my skills from them. That's how I learned I could do the shed." She later hired on as a helper to the same contractors and, along with tricks of the trade, gleaned many a useful bit of well-aged lumber from their other remodeling jobs.

In February, she moved up among all the construction and lived on cornflakes and cold cuts until the following fall. When she finally got appliances into her redesigned old-fashioned kitchen, she couldn't even wait to finish the wide pine floorboards. "It was like— I've got to cook real food." The floor has yet to see a finish other than Butcher's wax, but the cook has moved from plain, hot food to playing with fun things such as lavender ice cream and exotic salad greens. Deal's adventures with the mother of all fixer-uppers, so closely entwined in her garden's development, is a story for another time. The now-snug white farmhouse sits below the ridge where the road runs, surrounded by old lilacs, rugosa

Although delphiniums are a specialty, a wide variety of other blossoms are harvested from Debbie Deal's cutting gardens each year.

roses, and hollyhocks. A brick path bordered by spice-scented dianthus and culinary herbs curves to the front door.

The shed, which became her farm stand, Deal calls the first major test of her life. It was an old lobster trap workshop, full of culch and crumbling into the ground. She had it jacked up and re-silled and got somebody to skid it up to the roadside. "I'd never built anything in my life," she admits. "I replaced about seventy percent of the boarding, reframed it, put win-

dows in, did everything. It took me a whole season to complete the silly thing. Then I had to make a hard and fast decision. What was I going to do with it? It was really scary." She opted for raising vegetables to sell, and in due course the simple, gray-boarded little building has come into its own.

Old blue spatterware basins and kettles display tempting heaps of garden-fresh vegetables and huge bouquets of cut flowers. Deal put legs on an old dough trough and fills it

Debbie Deal's Delphiniums

with dewy ears of corn. "Atmosphere!" she declares. Many of the antiques that decorate the stand are left over from a time when Deal was an avid collector. She sold some at first, but the garden soon demanded all her attention. An old bean thresher, still in mint condition, actually works, and the cider press sees annual action. "One nice day every fall," she relates, "We go to [an orchard in] Hope or scrounge around here for apples. Then we come back and have a big picnic and press cider the whole day. It's lots of fun." Anyone who comes along is welcome to join in.

"Where I come from, their idea of gardening was putting a geranium on the doorstep."

Down beside the barn, where the shed once sagged, stands the greenhouse, which Deal has found indispensable. "It got to the point where it was becoming too expensive to buy plants, and after I moved the shed, my next project was a greenhouse. It turned out to be the hardest thing I ever did. I started so late in the fall, and the thing came with no instructions." She assembled the double plastic, hoop-style structure herself while autumn winds whipped around her. In it she grows everything for her fields and gardens as well as some for landscapers and other people. Except for new varieties she wants to try, most of the seeds she sows she has saved from her own plantings, for purposes of economy and certainty of results.

"My whole experience here is loads of fun," Deal says happily, "but it's also loads of work, because I have no help." She lives alone with her yellow Lab, Jessie, who helps out in her own way as watchdog and constant companion. "The easy part is that I have nothing else to distract me, so I can really focus on it." With the sale of her house in Massachusetts and other sources of income, she has been able to manage without getting in the hole. "I couldn't live off what [the business] makes. It makes me wonder how a lot of people do it. My business is definitely building in all respects, but it takes time for people to find you, know you exist." Deal goes with the flow of market demand. "One year it's more landscapers, another year it's more restaurants. I just try to keep flexible. I didn't come here with some big business plan. I know what they're all about, and, boy, was I getting away from *them*."

Deal's college major was art, and she taught art for several years before going into the business world. "It's so wonderful to be here," she reflects. "The best part is, I'm a visual person, so when I look at things, I get a lot of satisfaction from seeing just what's been created here . . . from looking out at the water . . . and just plain dreaming."

Heather Blooms at High Tide

Since 1992, when this article appeared in Down East, *Greta Waterman has closed her heather garden as a business but not as a continuing personal pleasure. She has been expanding her collection of dwarf conifers and experimenting with other plants that add interest to a heather garden. Her knowledge of heathers and advice on their culture remains as invaluable now as when the article was written.*

Just when we think we've said the last farewell to bright-blooming summer, as gold and bronze chrysanthemums fade in gardens and purple roadside asters have turned to tawny fluff, October pulls its neatest trick. With the first hard frost, modest little heathers, which have been biding their time in their softly varied green foliage and tiny pastel blooms, burst into a blazing tapestry of scarlet, orange, gold, copper, and maroon in a growing number of gardens across Maine.

It's thanks to people like Greta Waterman, a pioneer in introducing them in Maine, that heathers have become a favorite with gardeners on the coast and inland alike. Waterman has been studying and propagating them for the past eighteen years at her seaside home beside the Harraseeket estuary in Freeport. At The Heather Garden, as she calls her small retail nursery business, she grows more than a hundred varieties and raises two thousand plants a year for gardeners across Maine and New England.

Greta Waterman's fascination with these remarkable miniature shrubs began some twenty years ago, before she came to Maine. She credits her husband, George, a marine contractor, with fostering her love of plants. "He's the one who introduced me to the rose-marys," she explains. "His mother was an herbologist." Greta trained as a lab technician, specializing in electron microscopy. "It was very technical, and I worked with plant material," she says. "I learned the skills of controlled experiment, which I still use when I propagate plants." When the Watermans moved to Maine in 1974, the closest electron

KEVIN SHIELDS

Spectacular miniatures, heathers are at their most colorful in autumn.

microscope was in Boston, so she looked for another career, one she could pursue at home with her young children.

Heather seemed just right for her. "I like plants that are in miniature," she says. "I don't like big, showy ones. I love the little ones that have little flowers and fairly small growth habits." It may have something to do with her work in the microscopic world, which could also account for her interest in the technical side of her project, she speculates.

"I got into heathers in a big way about eighteen years ago, and it's just evolved," Waterman says. "I'm very noncompetitive. I like things I can do at my own pace." She helped found the Northeast Heather Society, a chapter of the North American Heather Society, and has served as its president. She

The heathers in Greta Waterman's coastal garden can survive repeated drenchings of salt water. They do need to be protected from drying winter winds, however.

The Grand Masters of Maine Gardening

helped noted Maine gardener David Emery start the well-known heather garden at Mrs. L. C. Smith's Wolf Neck Farm, now owned by the University of Maine, and continues to assist with its care. She also volunteers in the maintenance of Bowdoin College's extensive heather garden. But she says such activities are peripheral to her real interest, her own garden.

The color and diversity of heathers hold extraordinary appeal for Greta Waterman, as the plantings around her charming old house and its shoreline rock gardens attest. For all heather's myriad forms and colors, however, it is actually a single species with numerous varieties. In August and September most of these produce small, delicate blossoms in soft shades of pink and lavender, rose and purple, but their foliage and growth habits are more colorful and varied than their modest bloom. What follows the blossoms, after the first hard frost, is a ground-level display to rival that of the scarlet maples, golden aspens, and bronze oaks above. What's more, the heathers aren't deciduous like the trees. Their feathery foliage, in its autumn colors, hangs on to brighten the grays and browns of winter, a property that endears them to year-round gardeners, especially in climates more temperate than Maine's.

Here the foliage remains colorful all winter, but it is seldom possible to enjoy it for that long because snow usually buries the plants. Even if it doesn't, heathers need heavy protection to survive the blast of drying winter winds. But the extra work they require is well worth the effort, Waterman insists.

Heathers can range in height from ground-hugging prostrate forms to as tall as twenty-four inches. Some are compact, some are open, some conical, some bun-shaped. And they can be pruned to any desired height or shape. But the outstanding ingredient in heather's effect is its striking foliage color— not just in the fall, but all season long.

Varieties are sometimes named for the color of their foliage—for example 'Golden Feather' and 'Arran Gold'. Many of the golds retain their summer color in the fall; some turn reddish. The names 'Blazeaway' and 'Wickwire Flame' refer to these varieties' autumn display. Like most of the heathers that turn brilliant red and orange, their summer color is green, often the more limey shades. Some greens turn very little. Others, such as 'Durfordii', darken to a purplish hue, or even near black, such as 'Black Beauty'. 'Pink Tips' is named for its new spring growth, 'Rubrum' for its deep rose blossoms. But there's no regular pattern for the nomenclature. 'White Knight' has lavender blossoms and gray leaves. Gray-foliaged heathers are generally gray year-round and come through Maine winters especially well, according to Waterman.

Heathers offer wide-ranging opportunities to adventurous gardeners. Some people prefer to create a patchwork carpet solely of heathers. Particularly suitable for rock gardens, the plants can also be grown in pockets in ledge, where their spreading branches will cover a wide area from a single stem. Here, however, extra care must be taken to keep them from drying out. Heathers can be interspersed with other plants such as azaleas and rhododendrons, which require the same acid soils. Other plants that thrive in these soils, including alpine *Lewisia*, Japanese maples, dwarf conifers, and brooms (*Genista*), can lend an interesting variety of height and texture among the diminutive heathers.

One such plant that is often mixed—and confused—with heather (*Calluna*) is heath (*Erica*), which is considerably trickier to grow in Maine. Heaths bud up in fall and blossom the following spring. Their flowers are gen-

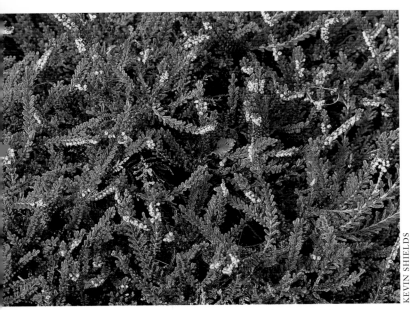

Heather flowers, though tiny, add even more textural interest to the fascinating foliage.

erally a striking white, rose, or purple. A very cold winter will jeopardize the bloom, however. "The buds have to go through winter successfully," says Waterman. "If we have a hard winter, they'll get blasted, and there will be no bloom at all the next season." Waterman does grow a few heaths in very sheltered spots, but she advises against trying to mix them with heathers. "I find that neither the heathers nor the heaths show off very well in a mix," she says.

As for the heathers themselves, Waterman prefers to plant the coppers and oranges and golds and reds among the deep greens and grays. "To have all colored foliage would look very strange, but splashes of color among the greens give you a nice contrast," she explains.

Heathers are especially favored for seaside gardens. "It's very important for people to know that they're salt-tolerant," Waterman says. Her raised beds are only a few yards from the shore of the Harraseeket estuary. "My gardens have been submerged in salt water for as long as five hours any number of times and have survived. I can also testify that heathers will tolerate salt spray." Wind is heather's worst enemy, and dealing effectively with it is the first priority for success with heathers in Maine.

"Some people on the coast say, 'If that variety isn't going to survive by itself, I won't grow it,'" Waterman notes. "I preach that all varieties of heather need to be covered. For me, that's usually after Thanksgiving, once the ground is partially frozen and all the rodents have found another place to live." The small animals will nest in the heathers and live there all winter under the mulch, chewing holes in the plants. Inland, where there's a more reliable snow cover, mulching isn't as crucial. The real devastation comes in February and March, when the snows have gone along the coast and the raw, desiccating onshore winds burn the foliage.

Pine needles, with their acid content, have long been the mulch of choice for heathers, but often it's difficult to give larger plants the complete coverage they need. "You have to put enough needles on them so you wouldn't even know the plants were there," Waterman says. Evergreen boughs, which are more open, are less effective.

Along with wind protection, regular pruning is essential to successful heather culture. Mulch should not be removed until mid-April along the Maine coast, or even later if the month remains wintry. About a week after uncovering the plants, when they have gotten used to the spring air, it's time to cut off all that nicely covered foliage. No leaves will grow where the plants blossomed the previous year, and removing the extra shrubbery not only improves the appearance of the plant but keeps plants healthier and more resistant to fungal diseases.

The best time to plant heather is spring, particularly in Maine, Waterman advises. The plants need the full growing season to get well established and become toughened to the environment before cold weather sets in. "Some people plant in August, but I would rather increase the chance of success by waiting till spring. I'm trying to train people to have optimum success. Heather has gotten a bad name, and a lot of nurseries won't carry it. But they don't educate people when they buy it."

Heathers don't mind the heat. And they require a certain amount of humidity, as long as the air is moving, which is one reason they do well on the coast or in alpine settings, Waterman says. Because they prefer acid, peaty soil light enough for their fine root system to penetrate (they don't thrive in clay), they often need to be watered—particularly if planted on ledge. Six to eight inches of soil is necessary to hold enough moisture for heather's shallow roots.

Moisture is also retained by mulching, which should be done as soon as they're planted. Come the next spring, some of the winter pine needle cover can be shaken down under the plants and only the excess removed.

For all heather's myriad forms and colors, it actually is a single species with numerous varieties.

Heather also needs at least a half-day of full sunlight. Waterman doesn't fertilize her heathers once they're in the ground.

She also doesn't advertise, relying mostly on gardeners talking to other gardeners to reach prospective customers. "I enjoy the process of growing heathers, I delight in people coming and buying them," she says, "but it's still mostly word of mouth." For years she has offered heathers as one- and two-year-old plants, but with the increasing demand for larger ones, she is now also selling older specimens. "This year I raised my prices because I've been harassed for not charging enough," she confesses. At three, four, and six dollars for the large ones, she says her prices are competitive with nurseries that grow them in greater volume.

And if she is not exactly getting rich with her business, running The Heather Garden does have its satisfactions. "I feel I have a niche and a knowledge that's fairly unique, because most people in Maine still don't know too much about heathers," she says. "And it gives me a great deal of pleasure knowing I have knowledge that I can pass on to others who want it."

Old Sheep Meadows
Grows Roses for Maine

Raymond and Michal Graber are among the most successful growers of roses in Maine, providing for gardeners in our challenging climate that essential element without which no garden is complete.

Visit Old Sheep Meadows Nursery in Alfred anytime in spring, summer, or early fall and it might as well be June, the traditional Month of Roses. All through the growing season, blooming roses fill spacious beds, ramble over stone walls, and climb high above eight-foot trellises. In the elegant display gardens, peonies, foxgloves, delphiniums, and other favorite perennials mingle felicitously with June-blooming heirloom roses and many more of the newer varieties that continue the summerlong show.

"We're devoted to roses. They're an important part of our lives," says Raymond Graber, who with his wife, Michal (pronounced *My*-chall), has been growing roses for Maine gardens at Old Sheep Meadows for more than forty years. "I have four hundred rose bushes out there. I cannot deal with a rosebush that's sick. A rosebush has to be hardy, healthy, tolerate my climate. If it can't do that, I don't need it. There are tens of thousands of roses, infinite varieties. So we just keep sorting through till we find those that live with us happily. And that's what we sell."

The Grabers have developed a plant list of about two hundred roses that can take Maine winters. Each year they offer between fifty and a hundred different selections, depending on what is available from suppliers and what Raymond raises from cuttings. Some of the old classics, many of the popular rugosas, and roses developed in Canada and Iowa are hardy to Zone 4, or –30 degrees. The David Austin roses, developed by the renowned English grower for their repeat bloom and splendid variety of color and form, vary in hardiness. Many do very well at Old Sheep Meadows, where mini-climates range from Zone 5 (coastal) to Zone 4 (inland) in the hillside location.

Michal, a full-time gardener herself, also creates gardens for clients of her landscape design business, Cape Cod Gardens. "I designed a rose garden for a lady in Millinocket. We sell to people in the White Mountains, Laconia, North Conway. They all do well," she says. People are amazed to learn that they don't have to take climbers down from their arbors in winter. "Just leave them up there. They won't winterkill," she tells them.

When the Grabers first got interested in roses, they followed the directions in all the books but still were not very successful. "The writers had pictures of their lovely gardens, so I knew *they* could grow roses. Why were *we* having so much trouble?" Raymond wondered. "Then one day a lightbulb came on. I looked at the books and saw they were growing roses in milder climates, England, California, the Carolinas. Where were the people from the

North? Why weren't *they* writing?" A plant ecologist (retired from the University of New Hampshire in 1990), he decided to apply his scientific know-how. Today there are many good books about northern roses that confirm what he learned through years of experimenting, he says. This information is shared with anyone who purchases roses at Old Sheep Meadows.

Hardiness is a must for growing roses successfully in Maine, but equally important is good soil. "If you can raise an excellent vegetable garden, you can grow roses," Michal insists. "You can't grow vegetables on compacted earth. You need air space for the roots to grow properly and for the earthworms to till it. Don't walk in your garden. Make a path or lay stepping stones." The Graber soil formula is one-third peat moss, one-third old manure, one-third topsoil. "The topsoil can be sandy," she says, "but if you have clay, you have to raise [the bed] way up. Clay holds the water, and roses don't like wet roots in winter. Most of the beds here have been constructed with dump-truck loads of topsoil, peat moss, and manure."

Raymond learned the hard way how to prepare a perfect rose bed on the farm's glacial till. "I was going to dig out all the stone, thirty inches deep, and fill it with good soil. I filled a pickup with stones three times—spent the whole summer on one little bed. I'll never do that again." After that, he used the natural granite formations of the hillside and recycled stones from the miles of old walls in the farm's two hundred now-forested acres to construct raised beds. For one particularly lovely setting, he filled a space behind a stone outcrop and ran ramblers over the boulders against a screen of white birches, rhododendrons, and tall shrub roses. A September surprise, a white cyclamen, gleams in the shade of ancient pines

nearby. A native of Asia Minor, it has survived a Maine winter. "I'm thinking of putting in some more and developing a little grove," Raymond says. " It's such a beautiful spot. I've talked about having a little [artificial] brook winding down the hillside to a reflecting pool.

'John Davis' roses cover the steep slope behind the Grabers' barn.

I always have more plans than energy," he admits, grinning.

Rather than plant a rosebush with the graft a few inches above the soil surface, the conventional practice, the Grabers have learned to bury the graft four to six inches deep to prevent the vulnerable splice from freezing. "In a well-mulched bed," says Raymond, "the soil seldom freezes. Once it freezes, it stays frozen. Heavy mulches can make a huge difference in winters with lots of temperature variations." Alternate freezing and thawing is disastrous for many perennials, and mulching is a must for successful rose gardening in Maine. Experimenting with numerous mulch materials, the Grabers have found pine needles by far the best. Bark mulch should be avoided because it "waterproofs the soil," they say. By the same token, peat moss should always be thoroughly wetted before it is added to the garden. It absorbs many times its own weight in water, leaving the plants thirsty. "Pine needles are hollow, sealed at both ends," Raymond points out. "The hollow space makes wonderful insulation. They resist becoming saturated in winter and break down relatively slowly. And they look so natural on the ground—like walking in the forest." Despite popular belief, pine needles are no more acidic than the rain or the already acid New England soils, he observes. "All organic material breaks down into humic acids." His regimen includes a light liming before he puts down a new layer of pine needles for winter insulation, which in turn become the necessary organic material that keeps the soil healthy. No need to dig in the mulch in the spring, he says. "Earth-

The old idea that grafting roses onto superior root stock gives a better plant is losing favor.

worms do the heavy lifting, moving it down into the soil."

Michal adds that digging is actually harmful to roses. Tilling could injure their horizontal root system. She describes the process of readying roses for winter as building a little sand castle around each plant. "Pull the pine needle mulch back and mound six or seven inches of topsoil over the bush so it's not pyramidal but [straight-sided]. That stays on the bush forever. About the first of November, add more pine needles. In the spring, don't take it off if good growth is coming through. The garden will be happy to have all that mulch."

Roses should be fed in May, June, and July, but no later than the first of August. "You could have a killing frost by the thirty-first of August here," she points out. "You don't want to encourage new growth, which would not have time to harden." The same goes for pruning in late summer, which would tell the plants to grow. "And don't uncover too soon in spring. We have had twenty degrees in May." When all danger of frost is past, dead wood can be pruned. A well-mulched, winter-hardy rose probably will have very little dead wood. For fertilizer, Michal falls back on Yankee thrift. "Just go to the local feed store and buy 19-19-19. It's cheap and well balanced. You don't need special rose food either. You can use a combination of 15-30-15 in June to make more blossoms. Just follow directions, put it on the ground, and water it in." She warns against fertilizer that's sprayed from a hose-mounted container, because it can burn the foliage. Fish emulsions are all right, she says, but the Grabers don't find them necessary.

The other vital necessity for rose culture

KEVIN SHIELDS

"If you can grow an excellent vegetable garden, you can grow roses," Michal Graber asserts.

is sufficient water. Roses need approximately an inch of rain a week, which is not always forthcoming. After trying various methods of irrigation, the Grabers have found that a soaker hose that weeps water, circling the plants three to six inches below the surface, works best for them. In very hot, dry weather, they run irrigation for an hour or two every day—on timers so it's not forgotten among the multitude of gardening chores.

The Grabers try to garden as organically as possible. To meet their requirements, a rose should be reasonably disease-resistant.

Raymond sprays when necessary with old-time remedies such as lime sulfur and baking soda for black spot and powdery mildew. Fallen leaves and other debris are cleaned up regularly. "If you start with a clean bed, you have relatively few problems," Raymond says. For the ubiquitous enemy of roses, Japanese beetles, he has found that the milky spore treatment works for him, but only because of the isolated setting. "If you're in a typical suburban environment, with a neighbor on each side who does nothing, you get to share their beetles even if you've done the right

Delicate pink 'Finch' roses

bought their farm from Percy Smith. Smith was a descendant of the original owner, who received it as a land grant from the English Crown. They raised their seven now-grown children in the house built in 1772 by Elder Henry Smith, who also built the Four Corner Baptist Church in Waterboro. Under layers of wallpaper and other modernizations, they found pine paneling, original moldings, and Indian shutters. Restored, the old house was cozy but dark, with its small period windows. Recently they added a glassed and screened garden room surrounded by a curving, flower-bordered terrace, where they can enjoy the birds and garden vistas when they find a rare moment to relax.

Old Sheep Meadows Nursery began operating as a business in the 1970s. It was named for the pasture where the Grabers kept sheep for thirty years. The roses first grew in the flower garden until the sheep were moved across the road and their meadow became the extended rose garden. The sheep were given up altogether once the designated shepherds, the younger generation, went off on their own. Since then, the Grabers have added daylilies to their plant list.

The daylilies are Michal's project. She has about 750 named varieties, as well as those that Raymond hybridizes. Aiming to produce tetraploids with repeat bloom, she selects promising blooms to be crossed, starts the resulting seeds indoors, and pots them up as they grow larger. As they mature, they are planted in raised growing beds in the same soil mix and with similar irrigation systems as the other Old Sheep Meadows gardens. "These are from 1995 and '96," she says, indicating several robust clumps. "The little ones potted up are from hybridizing last year. Our goal is to create repeat-blooming daylilies with unusual flowers that bloom from early July into

thing." The right thing is to apply the milky spore powder just before it rains or, better still, while it is raining. "It's a living organism that will be degraded instantly by sunlight. To work, it must be washed into the soil immediately."

More than thirty years ago, the Grabers

October." With their great variety of color and form, daylilies are valued additions to the Old Sheep Meadow display gardens and to those Michal designs for others.

Roses, however, remain Raymond's major occupation. He grows rooted cuttings from suppliers around the country to marketable size and raises cuttings from his own roses. "Many of the roses people want aren't available from nurseries. I have a choice whether to try to raise them or not have them," he says. "We feel that our own-root roses are superior." The old idea that grafting roses onto superior root stock gives a better plant is losing favor. "A hundred years ago, when grandmother had a rose, she would take a slip off and give it to her daughter. Those roses were extremely hardy. You find them growing around old foundations," Raymond points out. Among his favorites are a white rambler from the old Quaker burying ground in Alfred that blooms all through July, draped over a stone wall, and a raspberry-colored rambler that is not commercially available.

People come to Old Sheep Meadows from all over New England starting in April to see the spread of daffodils, during May to view the early daylilies, and all summer to enjoy the roses and perhaps choose irresistible specimens for their own gardens. The Grabers are not set up for mail order but will ship items that are purchased at the nursery. They have a small amount of seasonal help from a neighboring friend but do most of the work themselves.

The Old Sheep Meadows brochure invites gardeners to visit anytime but "especially during the peak of bloom from mid-July to the end of August." The annual Rose Open House lasts from June 12 through July 4. See Appendix for more information.

Wild Roses for the Garden

Wild roses are the progenitors of an almost infinite variety of elegant hybrids, many of which do well in Maine's northern climate. But wild roses in their natural state, from the familiar beach rose, Rosa rugosa, *to less commonly known species, can also be employed to great advantage in many garden and landscape situations. Adventurous gardeners will be rewarded for seeking them out. Suzy Verrier, cited in this 1993 article, has moved her business to North Creek Farm in Phippsburg.*

Glossy catalogs every winter herald the year's latest roses, preternaturally showy confections of color and form created in top laboratories and greenhouses. Mainers succumb to these slick blandishments probably in the same proportion as gardeners everywhere, but many I know discovered long ago that a half-dozen exotic hybrid tea roses can require roughly the same amount of time and care as a good-size garden of hardy perennials.

Our climate doesn't often favor fancy roses, but our insects almost universally do. Several Maine gardeners I've talked with say they actually treat tea roses as annuals and fully expect to replace most of them every year—hardly an exercise in Yankee thrift. But there's an alternative to being led down this dubious garden path. Happily, it's right under our noses.

All we have to do is stop and smell the wild roses that grow so abundantly on our beaches and islands, along our roads, in our bogs and upland pastures, more elegant in their natural simplicity than any "improved" commercial imitation. Wild roses are an apt metaphor for Maine: rugged, beautiful, sensible, adaptable. They're also the clue to growing virtually care-free roses in gardens from Kittery to Fort Kent.

The most visible of Maine's "wild" roses is *Rosa rugosa*, variously called the beach rose or the rugosa rose, which forms dense, six-foot-high thickets. Its bright pink blossoms fill the seaside or inland meadow air with heady fragrance in June. Its crab-apple–size scarlet hips are an autumn display to anticipate. Rugosas also come in white; there's a magnificent cliffside patch of them near the Owls Head Light, just south of Rockland. But rugosas, like many respectable inhabitants of Maine, are actually "from away." Originally from Asia, they came to New England from Europe in the nineteenth century and proved so happy here that they quickly escaped and naturalized in the countryside. Even though they can't qualify as true natives, "You'd really have to call them a wild rose," concedes Suzy Verrier, who specializes in old and hardy roses at her Forevergreen Farm nursery. "Go to any little island off the coast, and you'll find them. Certainly they weren't planted in those spots." And just as certainly, on an island or inland, they're a permanent aspect of the Maine scene.

Who could capture the essence of wild roses in a Maine summer better than Celia

Thaxter, the popular poet and garden writer of a century ago? She loved the wildflowers of her otherwise barren Appledore Island as much as the blooms she carefully nurtured in her famous garden. She mentions them frequently in her classic *An Island Garden:* "Beyond the garden, the green grassy spaces sloping to the sea are rich with blossoming thickets of wild roses, among the bleached white ledges, blushing fair to see, and the ocean beyond shimmers and sparkles beneath the touch of the warm south wind."

Celia doesn't tell us whether her wild roses are beach roses or "pasture roses," which thrive just as well in similar settings. A true North American native is *Rosa virginiana.* It has slightly larger blossoms than its cousin *Rosa carolina,* which prefers a somewhat moister habitat. Both have long, branching canes and delicate single flowers. There are finer distinctions between the two for the dedicated botanist, but for the rest of us, both offer the same simple joy of encountering a wild rose—preferably at a safe distance, for their thorns are murderous to the unwary wanderer or the too-intent berry picker.

It was doubtless one of these pasture roses, the "sweet single rose of New England," that is said to have cheered the homesick Pilgrims, so closely does it resemble the English sweetbrier, *Rosa eglanteria,* or eglantine. Nathaniel Hawthorne, with studied symbolism, placed a "wild rose-bush, covered this month of June with its delicate gems," beside the prison door through which Hester Prynne, wearing her scarlet letter, passed to her fate. Shakespeare included the eglantine among the more than seventy mentions of roses of all kinds in his plays and sonnets. Indeed, the sweetbrier is another of the imports in succeeding centuries that has escaped from old-fashioned gardens into the wild. Some giant

RAND RAABE

Best known of Maine's wild roses is Rosa rugosa, *which actually originated in Asia.*

specimens thrive at the historic Pettengill Farm, maintained by the local historical society in Freeport.

Wildflower literature lists several other native roses, all of which have single pink flowers similar to the pasture roses. The swamp rose, *Rosa palustris,* has hooked thorns and dwells in wetlands. The northeastern rose, *Rosa nitida,* whose canes, we are warned, are "densely prickled with dark purple bristles," is also a bog lover. *Rosa blanda,* the smooth rose, in contrast is nearly thornless and prefers rocky slopes and shores. A diligent naturalist can ferret out and accurately identify these variations on the rose theme with the aid of a good manual such as the Peterson *Field Guide to Wildflowers* or Marilyn Dwelley's *Summer & Fall Wildflowers of New England.*

But, more to our purpose, here is just what this bouquet of wild roses has to tell the Maine gardener. First of all, roses, the backbone of any old-fashioned or cottage garden, are definitely possible to grow in our climate, and they don't require undue amounts of time or care to cultivate. Anyone who can grow a delphinium or a Shasta daisy can grow wild roses. The pasture rose is a favorite with David Emery, a well-known southern Maine landscape gardener. "It's so simple, so adaptable," he says. "It's happy in shallow soil and at dry sites. It does well in shade. I love its hips even more than the rugosa's because they last so long, and the red canes are beautiful in winter." Emery propagates *Rosa virginiana*, which blooms later than the rugosa, and uses it in landscaping, often as a ground cover in difficult areas.

Suzy Verrier seconds Emery on the value of this rose for its attractive shrubby clumps, its willingness to thrive in clay soil, and its salt and wind tolerance. "It's also great," she says, "because it blooms in late July and August, when nothing much is happening with other roses. And its deep red fall foliage is superb." In addition to this pasture rose, she recommends two other European wild roses. *Rosa wichuraiana* is a low-growing variety that has naturalized in Maine and makes a good ground cover. Scotch, or burnet, rose *(Rosa spinosissima)*, which was popular at the turn of the last century, has also spread to the wild, partly because its prolific hips are fancied by birds and chipmunks. "It's one of the best wild roses," Verrier says. It's salt tolerant and has very dense, delicate foliage, and fine thorns that make it easier to handle. It produces beautiful clumps of very early white blossoms, whose fragrance carries on the air. The foliage turns dark red in the fall and its hips are black rather than the usual red.

Our other alien wild rose grows as tall as the rugosa but otherwise is quite different. *Rosa multiflora* has arching seven-foot canes that form huge mounds covered with tiny white flowers rather resembling blackberry blossoms. Long-lasting when picked and intensely fragrant, the flowers can fill a house with their perfume. In autumn, the little clusters of bright orange hips are attractive to birds and popular material for wreaths, outlasting most of the other winter berries. A native of the Orient, the multiflora, which has apparently never earned a common name, has run wild chiefly because it was used a lot as rootstock for other roses, Verrier explains. "If roses aren't planted deep enough, they may lose their top stock and then the rootstock produces its own kind." Quite a number of cultivated ramblers and climbers have been developed from the multiflora, and thereby hangs a tragic tale, according to Verrier. A disease called rose rosette, fatal to the wild multifloras, has been spreading from the Midwest in our direction. "If it gets here and affects the wild multifloras," Verrier warns, "it will then start affecting roses with multiflora background. The only way I can think to prevent it is to not plant multifloras and probably to destroy the ones in the wild."

How can Maine gardeners take advantage of wild roses? First of all, learn more about the rugosas. (Rugosa, by the way, means wrinkled, referring to the plant's very crinkly leaves.) Hundreds of elegant rugosa hybrids have been developed from the original species: every shade in the white to deep red spectrum, singles, doubles, varied in shape and habit. Suzy Verrier has written a small book about these roses, *Rosa Rugosas* [1991, distributed by Firefly Books, Buffalo, N.Y.], and in it she describes them all as "wind and salt tolerant, disease resistant, chemical free and cold hardy." In short, many rugosa hybrids retain the best qualities of the wild variety. Rugosa hybrids as well as the species

The delicate pink buds of Rosa rugosa alba *open to pure white blossoms.*

(or wild) rugosas are available at many Maine nurseries and garden centers.

As for the other wild roses, some of those are also available from nurseries. Verrier strongly advises against digging them or any other wild plants in their native habitat. "It's become very much a horticultural 'no-no,'" she says. "Even if there are lots of them, someone else could come in and take them on a commercial basis and wipe them out." In addition, in the case of roses, digging them up in the wild usually does not work. The shoots and runners don't have proper roots, and the plants often die as a result of the transplanting. Digging them up only disturbs the original clump and is likely to spread disease.

"The best thing to do is to take some hips and start some young plants," advises Verrier. "Roses come true from seed, and they're not hard to grow. You'll get a better plant than from trying to transplant one from the wild. Growing a rose from seed doesn't take long, either. You can have a good-size bush in three years."

But three years is a long time. The time to start looking for wild roses and learning about them, whether or not you plan to put them in your garden, is in June and July, when they blossom most prolifically. Those are the weeks to wander in search of their delicate beauty, adorning the sun-drenched emptiness of upland pastures or the barren sands and ragged ledges of the shore, to reflect upon the peculiar poignancy of the wild rose, with its perfume and its prickle, its ability to survive the ravages of time and tempest, like so many other native and naturalized residents of Maine.

Tom York's Rhododendrons

Rhododendrons are wonderful shrubs that are not always thought of as important, or even easy, to include in the Maine landscape. Tom York has made significant progress in dispelling this myth. He has continued to enlarge and refine his rhododendron collection and his nursery business in the three years since this profile was originally published. Though he visited and consulted with the late Roger Luce, he doesn't offer any Luce cultivars for sale.

For the folks who think of rhododendrons only as those large, magenta-flowered, leather-leaved denizens of metropolitan suburbs to the south, it will come as a surprise that there are perhaps twelve to fifteen thousand named varieties of this shrub. They come in an astonishing assortment of shapes, sizes, and exquisite colors, and perhaps a hundred and fifty of them can be successfully grown in Maine.

At York's Hardy Rhododendrons in West Bath, Tom York cultivates "a small percentage of the total, but a pretty good representation of a lot of the varieties." From April to mid-July, they flaunt their fountains of pink and white, peach and yellow, rose and lavender, crimson and maroon with lavish abandon in an informal landscape display that suggests in microcosm the world-famous Winterthur Gardens in Delaware. But York is no scion of the DuPonts. He grew up next door to his nursery and built his house on old family farmland, later expanding his gardens onto property purchased from a neighbor. Always an after-hours gardener, he took early retirement in 1992 from Bath Iron Works, where he was director of facilities, to try to start a nursery business.

"It was a hobby that got out of control," York says. "The kids had left the nest, and it gave me time to work on [the business]." The hobby began earlier, when he bought three 'English Roseum' rhododendrons and noticed there was a variation in their shades of pink, though they were supposed to be identical plants. His curiosity aroused, he began reading about them and found there were many variations, some hardy in Maine. "It became a challenge to find out if I could grow them," he says. He joined the state rhododendron society and met a lot of people "originally from New Jersey." His search for Maine-hardy rhododendrons soon became an obsession. He admits to a lot of failures, but at the same time he has found many that do well here. With a background in engineering, York had no formal botanical training or experience in raising rhododendrons in containers for retail sale, a process he says he learned "as my own apprentice."

A visitor to the display garden eventually strolls down the hillside to the business end of the operation. Outside a cluster of greenhouses stand neat rows of potted rhododendrons, azaleas, mountain laurel, and even magnolias in successive stages of growth, their seductive colors tempting the bemused gardener to extravagant visions—from small improvements to total reconstruction of the home landscape. York confirms the practicability of their dreams as he extols the scope and versatility of these remarkable shrubs.

Though most peak from late May to early June in Maine, there are rhododendrons of Siberian ancestry that bloom as early as April, and summer azaleas that flower as late as mid-July. *Rhododendron maximum*, a large, white-flowered native species found in the wild in a carefully guarded Maine preserve, is sometimes discovered blooming in August. Rhododendrons range from rock-garden-size dwarfs to six- to eight-foot giants. Indeed, in moist, temperate climes such as the Pacific Northwest, rhododendrons reach the height of small trees, and centuries-old specimens on Irish estates can have trunks nearly a foot in diameter. There are evergreen and deciduous, large-leaved and small-leaved varieties of both rhododendrons and azaleas, to say nothing of the wondrous array of blossom shapes and colors, as well as decorative foliage.

With such a smorgasbord to choose from, it's no exaggeration to say there's something for every garden situation. "It's important to recognize that there is a long bloom period," York says. "It gives you a chance to do a lot of planning. There's a great range of plants that look nice [with rhododendrons and their kin]—hostas, ferns, astilbes, dwarf conifers, flowering crabs, daffodils, tulips, if the deer don't get them."

The colors of 'Casanova' (top), 'Sham's Candy' (right), and 'Percy Wiseman' blend compatibly in Tom York's rhododendron garden.

Tom York's Rhododendrons

Conifers and woodland plants partner well with rhododendrons and azaleas.

York delights in pointing out each plant's special attributes. "The best early-season rhododendron is *dauricum* 'Album'. It's deciduous, has clear white flowers, and blooms with the daffodils." There are several selections, varying in height from two to six feet, and it's generally hardy to –25 to –30 degrees. 'Cornell Pink', another winter-tough one, blooms at the same time. Mid-season varieties are the most numerous. Besides the old standbys that are still very popular in Maine—'English Roseum' in many shades; the big, white *catawbiense* 'Album', a late-season variety; the ubiquitous near-red 'Nova Zembla'—there are startling oranges such as 'Hindustan'; luscious peaches and lemony yellows; the dwarf scarlet 'Baden Baden', which gleams provocatively along a shaded woodland path; the exotic 'Calsap', its orchid-like white flowers marked with a deep maroon eye; the hardy 'Scintillation', a charmer with ruffled pink flowers and large, shiny leaves; and dozens more with their own unique appeal. There's an endless procession of new hybrids, including an interesting series from Finland.

Deciduous azaleas, which are winter-hardy, unlike the supermarket "Mother's Day" sort, are characterized by a wide range of colors—pastels, light yellows, oranges, reds—York points out. Mountain laurel, whether originating in the cool Appalachian Mountains to the south or native to Maine, as is the well-known sheep laurel, does well here. Many of its blooms, with their little dimples and bands of red and white, or burgundy and pink, easily qualify it for the common name "calico bush." There are probably fifteen to twenty kinds of magnolias that thrive in Maine, of which York has seven or eight in his garden. 'Butterflies', a new, hardy yellow one with "great foliage," does especially well, he says.

The best news is that these elegant flora prefer a rather simple lifestyle. Their essential requirement is porous, well-drained, acidic soil—fairly typical in Maine. Clay soils should be avoided. "My soil is essentially all clay. That's why I have raised beds," York says, noting that one can resuscitate a languishing plant by digging around it, lifting it up, and putting good soil underneath to give it its own mini-raised bed. "Rhododendrons, once established, are pretty self-reliant. If you have the right soil to begin with, or amend it to make it right, they're essentially trouble free." Location is of primary importance, and plants should be selected accordingly, he says. A north-facing site, protected from winter sun and wind, is preferable, especially for large-leaved, evergreen plants, which are subject to serious drying. Small-leaved and deciduous plants are best for sunny or windy spots. Most varieties do well in partial shade or filtered light. A slope is ideal for rhododendrons and their relatives. Mountain laurel, especially, thrives on a steep hillside.

"Moist but not saturated" is the formula for watering these plants. For newly planted rhododendrons, once every seven to ten days is plenty, York says. The second year, after two to three weeks without rain, watering once is sufficient. "After that, they should be able to take care of themselves," he says. For soil, rhododendrons prefer a pH of about 6.5, which allows them to absorb nutrients. "My soil isn't very acidic, so I use fertilizers designed for acid-loving plants, high in sulfur and iron, with a few trace elements. They're not heavy feeders, but a little bit of fertilizer makes a big difference in the health of the plant. Magnolias like the same kind of soil, but a little richer."

York raises most of his plants from cuttings he roots himself or from rooted cuttings he buys in. After about nine months in a heated greenhouse, the plants are transferred to cold storage in unheated greenhouses, some of them under screening that provides partial shade. They move through a succession of larger pots, arriving at the two-gallon size, ready for sale, when they are three or four years old and mature enough to get established in a garden. Rhododendrons don't reach full hardiness until they're five or six years old. Prices range from $15 to $50 depending on size, variety, and age. Some dwarf plants can be six inches high at four years old, whereas some are three feet high at the same age. The age, not the size, governs the price.

"It's a long cycle, about four or five years from the time you start a plant until you sell it," York says. "It's surprising how similar a small nursery is to a large shipbuilding business. All the principles, the long-range planning that goes into ships, are common to raising trees and shrubs. It takes many years to launch them."

York's background in the shipbuilding

KEVIN SHIELDS

Pale pink 'Windbeam'

industry has stood him in good stead in designing his greenhouses, making business plans, and finding ingenious ways to maintain a family operation. His wife, Beth, helps with the mowing and weeding and runs the office. "Every corner I turn, it isn't something I already knew how to do. I'm always learning. It's almost like your first job. That's how exciting it is."

Maine's Rare Wild Rhododendrons

Rhododendrons, like asters and roses, grow wild in Maine, but unlike the latter two, they are seldom seen, except by the dedicated seeker. Mark Stavish, who provided some of the information for this 1992 article, has moved his nursery, Eastern Plant Specialties, to Clark, New Jersey.

Wild rhododendrons, those broad-leaved evergreens with massive rosy blooms, glorify springtime hillsides and forests from Connecticut to the Carolinas. Many people think that only their brightly colored cultivated cousins exist in Maine, gracing affluent suburban lawns or public gardens.

Not so, say knowledgeable wildflower enthusiasts. Maine boasts a small but handsome stand of the star of the family, *Rhododendron maximum* (great laurel, or rosebay rhododendron), sequestered in a hard-to-find spot in York County like some lost tribe as yet undiscovered by civilization. And a lost tribe it may well be. The *Rhododendron maximum* in the Harvey Butler Memorial Rhododendron Sanctuary in Springvale, at the very edge of the species' northern range, may be survivors from periods of warmer climate in past centuries.

Roughly eight hundred species of rhododendrons and their relatives are native to the Northern Hemisphere, many of them growing on the lofty slopes of the Himalayas. Maine, too, is home to several more familiar but smaller, less glamorous members of the family—the deep magenta rhodora (*R. cana-dense*) that, "In May, when sea-winds pierce our solitudes," as Emerson tells us, spreads "its leafless blooms in a damp nook"; and the well-named calico bush or mountain laurel and its lesser cousin, the bright pink sheep laurel (lambkill), which clings to the ledges of rocky pastures and windswept offshore islands. In contrast to their more modest displays, the great laurel, at its peak in July, showers a splendor of pink and white flower clusters up to six inches across over dark, leathery greenery that often ascends fifteen feet toward the forest canopy above, the blossoms glowing like fallen stars amid the dappled shade.

The state's sole stand of these imposing wild rhodies is discreetly tucked out of sight. Following a trail that's well marked once the location of its unobtrusively labeled entrance is found, one crosses logs that span boggy rivulets and shortly enters a new atmosphere. The path climbs steeply, and a sign announces the Harvey Butler Memorial Rhododendron Sanctuary. "All of a sudden, the feel of the forest is very different, more like typical *maximum* territory in New Jersey or the Great Smokies," says Mark Stavish, of Eastern Plant Specialties in Georgetown. Stavish's nursery

> *"All of a sudden, the feel of the forest is very different."*

features a wide range of rhododendrons, and he's also studied them extensively in the wild. Stavish, like many other plant people and botanists, has tagged some of the Harvey Butler Sanctuary's most elegant blossoms for the purpose of collecting seed in fall. Among the many hybrids that have been developed from *Rhododendron maximum*, 'Summer Summit' and 'Summer Snow' are two that do especially well in Maine, he says. The Springvale location is ideal habitat, with its acid soil and north-facing slopes, forested with beech and hemlock, that dip toward a red maple swamp. Several of these knolls rise from the five-acre bog to form the main rhododendron stand. A few more specimens are scattered in isolated spots in the area.

The sanctuary is owned and maintained by the New England Wild Flower Society, Inc., with headquarters at Garden in the Woods, in Framingham, Massachusetts. The Maine chapter has an office at the Pine Tree State Arboretum in Augusta. Three other sanctuaries in Maine are owned by the society, as well as one each in New Hampshire, Vermont, and Massachusetts. For each one, a society member serves as a steward.

Nancy McReel, of Wells, is responsible for the Harvey Butler sanctuary. "The society's primary objective," she says, "is to protect and sustain the existing population of *Rhododendron maximum*, which is of interest to ecologists, horticulturists, botanists, and geobotanists." For the last, the special attraction is that this stand of great laurel is a "disjunct" population in an isolated area. McReel's main task is to visit the site every spring, armed with clippers and bow saw, to make sure the path is clear and to check the stand's condition.

Winter snowmobile traffic also helps keep the perimeter trail open. Fortunately, the terrain where the shrubs actually grow is too rough for snowmobiles to drive over, she says.

McReel is also custodian of a stack of literature and copies of old deeds that tell the sanctuary's story. Harvey Butler was a farmer who cut cordwood and pastured cows on the land surrounding the rhododendrons in the early 1900s. The stand was likely damaged to some extent by his operations before he died in 1941. His son, Francis, hoping to preserve the rare shrubs, sold forty-five acres encompassing the stand to the New England Wild Flower Society. Looking over the deeds in her Wells living room, McReel notes that there's no date of purchase, only the usual "for one dollar and other valuable considerations…" and the stipulation: "The grantors reserve the right to enter upon said premises and remove therefrom a small quantity of rhododendron roots for their own immediate use during their respective lives."

KEVIN SHIELDS

Rhododendron Maximum *is the wild progenitor of many of the gorgeous hybrids that flourish in Maine gardens.*

Great laurels reach high for the sun on wooded knolls that rise from a Sanford bog.

"I don't know if they ever did," McReel says. She guesses the deed dates from the 1940s or 1950s. Another deed, dated 1964, provides for a ten-foot right-of-way to access the sanctuary. There's also a stand of rhododendrons designated the William B. Plummer

Memorial Rhododendron Sanctuary. Plummer died in 1918, and the land he left was purchased sometime later from his heir, apparently to complete the protected site.

In 1977 the Harvey Butler sanctuary was deemed important enough to be added to the state's list of "areas containing or potentially containing plant and animal life or geological features worthy of preservation in their natural condition or other natural features of significant scenic, scientific, or historical value." At one time the New England Wild Flower Society was reluctant to let the public know about Maine's unique rhododendrons. "But it seems to be such a healthy stand," McReel says, "and they realize that only people truly interested in seeing these beautiful plants would go all that distance. The fear of digging and vandalism has decreased."

Mark Stavish isn't so sure. "That stand is very fragile," he says. "It's not reproducing freely. It's suffering from two dry summers and severe deer pressure. Around the edges the lower six feet [of the shrubs] are bare where the deer have chewed off the branches." Nevertheless, he says, the stand is remarkable. "Having looked at thousands upon thousands of *Rhododendron maximum* in New Jersey and the Poconos and the Smokies, I can say these are by far the larger and better forms. The flowers are bigger than most, and even though the stand itself is not doing well, the ones that are there are clearly superior forms."

The Harvey Butler Memorial Rhododendron Sanctuary is open to qualified groups and individuals for scientific use, study, and inspection. Organized groups are preferred. For more information see Appendix.

The Grand Masters of Maine Gardening

The Sawyers Light Up the Shade

Rick and Gail Sawyer have met the challenge facing many gardeners: how to make shady areas really interesting. At Fernwood, hostas are the specialty, but they offer hundreds of other choices of plants that thrive in the shade. Rick is a true disciple of the late Roger Luce, from whom he learned about many of them. He helped Roger hybridize and propagate and is now sharing the care of the Luce horticultural legacy with Roger's sister, Eleanor Hardy.

A tapestry of outsize hostas spills down the pine-shaded hillside entrance like a Henri Rousseau jungle painting. Their variety of color, shape, and texture is impressive enough, but the fact that these giants, some spreading as wide as seven feet, have relatives with leaves as tiny as a thumbnail is nothing short of astonishing. And that's only the beginning of what a visitor discovers at Fernwood Nursery and Gardens in Swanville, where Rick and Gail Sawyer raise a host of woodland and shade-loving plants, many of them rare or at least seldom heard of.

A passion for hostas was the starting point ten years ago, when the Sawyers began carving the nursery out of the woods around their house. Ferns came next, and the procession of wild and cultivated perennials quickly lengthened into the neat rows of plant material under shade cloth. This sales area is expanding into the surrounding woodsy borders, where Rick continues to thin the trees and make room for extra stock and propagation.

"I have no idea how many varieties we have," Rick admits. "Hundreds of hostas, forty varieties of ferns. Scores of different types of astilbes, *Pulmonaria*, Solomon's seal, anemones, primulas, orchids." Contrary to the popular conception, not all woodland wildflowers are spring-blooming. There are lilies, lobelias, anemones, *Heuchera*s (coral bells), and primulas (primroses) that bloom late in the season and some that even blossom "from frost to frost," as Rick puts it. The average gardener is familiar with most of the standard versions of these, but how many of them have seen an all-gold-leaved lily-of-the-valley or one with dark green and yellow-striped leaves or an Asian jack-in-the-pulpit that blooms in midsummer and produces a spectacular long, yellow spathe? There are plants that flourish in the difficult habitat of dry shade, such as bloodroot, wild ginger, and wintergreen, and even shade-tolerant grasses.

Native Maine plants rub shoulders with many "from away"—the American South and West, Europe, and Asia. "We do a lot of pushing the envelope, testing the limit of hardiness," Rick says. "We stick things in the garden to see if they survive. All the plants we grow are hardy to this area. We never mulch for winter. A lot of zone ratings of plants [given in books] are merely a guess. No one has really tried them in Maine." Although Fernwood, only four miles from Penobscot Bay, enjoys the moderating effect of the sea air flowing up the Goose River valley to Swan-

Hostas are noted for their great variety of foliage color, form, and size.

ville, supposedly delicate plants that the Sawyers have given to friends living much farther north have succeeded. "People should be encouraged to experiment," Rick says. "The best part of gardening is experimenting. It's what I enjoy most, trying something different."

A native of Auburn, Rick moved to Massachusetts in 1975 after finishing college, and started working in a nursery. "I started from the ground up, [became] a manager, and learned a lot the hard way. I killed a lot of plants," he says with a smile. He returned to Maine and met Gail, who is originally from Brewer. After several moves they eventually ended up in Swanville in 1988. They started the nursery in 1991, while Rick worked as a UPS driver. Two years ago he retired from that job to devote more than weekends to the nursery business.

"He was finally tired," Gail says. "We decided it was time for him to quit that and do what he really loves, because he's so good at it. He's the real plantsman and gardener. He's the brains behind the plants part of it. I do the paperwork and advertising." All the same, she loves the plants, too, and readily identifies them to customers strolling through the garden. Some plants have only Latin names, being too rare to have acquired common ones.

Except for a small vegetable garden, the house they purchased was completely surrounded by woods. "You couldn't even see the road from the house," Rick says. "We had to do a lot of thinning." They also had to build up the soil: "It was terrible. The roots and rocks were so thick we couldn't dig it, so we brought in loam, added compost and shredded leaves, and built it above the ground." Woodland plants do well in slightly acid soil, with a pH of 5.5 to 6.5, he says. Though not officially certified as organic, Fernwood's gardens flourish without the aid of chemical fertilizers. Rick maintains optimum soil quality with compost and manures, much to the surprise of some visitors, who can't believe that this method could produce such healthy plants. He purchases compost by the truckload from various producers in his area. "They use a lot of seafood by-products, leaves, sawdust, manures, spoiled hay, but we stay away from sludge," Rick points out. "I periodically top-dress with the stuff. It feeds plants from the top down, as it does in nature."

At the sunny center of the Fernwood scene lies a small pond, totally man-made. "We were told by the former owners that there might be a spring, but when we dug down, there was nothing," Rick notes. "We had to line it with rubber. We tried three kinds of clay, but it leaked every time." Surrounded by some of the rocks excavated in leveling the garden, the pond is "fed" by an artfully contrived waterfall that operates by means of a circulating pump. Pickerelweed and hardy pond lilies grace the surface. A depth of four to six feet is adequate

The display gardens flanking the entrance only hint at the enormous choice of plants available at Fernwood Gardens.

for their winter survival. Flowering trees and shrubs—dogwoods, magnolias, pussy willows, and others hardy in Maine—soften the pond's borders. Ferns fill crevices and hang lushly over ledges around the waterfall. A bog behind the pond is the 2001 project. "We'll put in a liner, fill the bottom with porous material that the water will go through, and top that with a peatlike soil to plant in. The plants will feed on the nitrates in the water and help to purify it, a sort of working wetland." The bog and its plantings will complete the garden's visual composition. Rick is often asked to design gardens for others, but politely declines.

The Sawyers like to let plants mix it up in the display gardens that surround the working area and the house. "We try to let things go and do what they're supposed to do," Rick explains. Dwarf astilbes, painted ferns, and the surprisingly shade-loving Japanese roof iris shelter beneath rain-forest-size *Peltoboykinia* (one of those which has no common name) with huge, umbrella-like leaves. Exotic as it appears, it's another import from north-temperate Japan that's quite happy in Maine. Hostas dominate the bank in front of the house, not only as a signature greeting to visitors but as a laboratory. "One thing you learn in this bed," says Rick, "is that some hostas are slug-resistant and some are not. Slugs have a selective taste. That one never gets eaten; this one does." Although most hostas are grown

Blooming at different times throughout the summer, feathery-blossomed astilbes offer a range of color from white to deep maroon.

for their endlessly varied foliage—crinkled, gray-green, striped—a few have noteworthy blossoms. The tall, lily-like flower of 'White Triumphator' is slightly fragrant. 'Elvis Lives' is an attractive blue. 'Kryptonite' is a darker shade. "All the hostas you see from that lamp post and most of the way down the hill are ones we have hybridized," Rick points out. "We have a couple on the market—'Jimmy Crack Corn', 'Reptilian', that one, called 'Tractor Seat'. (It does look like one. One of our customers named it, and we liked it so much we went with it.)" Rick always goes for the unusual: "There's such a thing as too many varieties of hostas. There are so many on the market that they [make] no practical difference in the landscape."

Rick hasn't studied plant science formally, but says he has made it up as he goes along. "It's sort of like a gathering. You keep gathering. If you have an interest in particular types of plants, you start trying to find them, gathering stock or sources till you get a compilation of those plants. A lot of the plants we're interested in are not readily available, if at all, on the market. So we have to acquire those plants and learn how to propagate them, which can be a challenge."

At the same time, the Sawyers find themselves constantly having to resist the temptation to grow. "It can be overwhelming," says Gail, "especially when one man does it all. Rick has no extra help. We might coerce a relative into doing a little weeding in trade for some plants, but we've made a decision to keep the place small enough so that Rick and I can handle it on our own." It means being selective, even getting rid of one thing to add another that's more important. The fun of making those choices is what keeps gardeners like Rick and Gail Sawyer on a lifelong quest.

"The best part of gardening is experimenting. It's what I enjoy most."

Bare Ledge Blossoms
for Phid and Sharon Lawless

Gardening in Maine usually means dealing with the state's granite underpinnings a foot or just inches under the soil, or even incorporating outcroppings into the landscape design. But has anyone made a garden in a virtually soil-less abandoned quarry? Phid and Sharon Lawless have.

They also have an indirect connection with the legendary Beatrix Farrand. Their business was inspired by the work of Eric Soderholtz, whose pots graced Farrand's Reef Point gardens. And like so many serious gardeners in Maine, they were friends of Roger Luce.

Visitors could once freely wander up the long drive, but they became so numerous that the Lawlesses eventually had to gate the road (which is now paved) to preserve their privacy. However, as Sharon points out, at the shop visitors can see a full display of pots in a landscape setting. Professional landscape designers may be offered a visit to the private grounds.

Phid and Sharon Lawless are one of those wise couples who have taken inspiration from Maine's provocative charms and challenges, satisfying their practical needs and their creative passions at the same time. One of their most impressive accomplishments is a garden on grounds almost entirely devoid of soil, a situation not uncommon at home sites on our ubiquitous foundation of stony ledge. Doubtless there are many solutions to this problem, but probably none as dramatic as turning an abandoned granite quarry into the hidden Eden at Lunaform in West Sullivan.

Lunaform is the name of the business that supports the Lawless lifestyle, which is in essence a dedication to the arts. Maine's reputation as a nourishing climate for artists—and for ingenious entrepreneurs—is well founded, and the Lunaform business seems to have grown as much from Sharon's need to garden as from Phid's need for artistic expression. The Quarry Garden, as they have named it, is

an integral part of a business as unique as its setting. The Lunaform studio produces elegant, hand-turned garden planters, pots, bowls, urns, and fountains using a patented steel-reinforced-concrete process.

"That's how I can garden on granite. I got my husband to start a great business and make me all kinds of beautiful pots so I could have flowers," Sharon Lawless says, with just a touch of mischief as she leads a visitor up the winding, wooded drive. Suddenly it opens into a bemusing tapestry of gray stone and spring green birch, oak, and wild cherry interwoven with dark conifers and forest shadows. Random splashes of bright-blooming flowers spill from big, classically simple pots. The whole lovely fabric is mirrored in placid sheets of sunlit water. Around the next bend appears another breath-taker, a high, rectangular house, its timber and stucco walls and broad, flaring roof declaring Phid's fondness for Japanese architecture. The artful stone foundation follows the rising curve of unbroken natural granite paving.

"It's pretty neat," says Sharon. "People used to come upon our house by accident, and it was always a sort of shock to drive up this woods road and see a Japanese house. It's actually situated on one of the old quarries, and this road is the one they used to ship the stone down to schooners on Taunton Bay. It was all cut cobblestone they sent to Boston, New York and Philadelphia. [Creating a garden here is] a wonderful thing to do with an abandoned quarry, [which otherwise is] just a hole in the woods where kids could fall in."

Actually, the house, designed by Phid and built eighteen years ago, is older than the business. The Lawlesses came to Maine in 1976 and operated a sporting goods store in Ellsworth for many years. They sold that eight years ago and started the pot business because Phid, an architect and sculptor, longed to be doing something more creative. "We've always loved beautiful garden pottery and could never find any, so my husband just decided to make some," Sharon explains. "He found out how, and it's been a huge success because, I'm assuming, a lot of other people haven't been able to find any either." Phid's inspiration was the work of Eric Soderholtz, who made beautiful urns and planters in his West Gouldsboro studio in the early 1900s. Among the Lunastone collection of original designs and historic reproductions is "Reef Point," a precise replica of a Soderholtz pot from a Beatrix Farrand garden. The reproduction is also available at the Thuya Garden in Northeast Harbor; sales of the pot help to support that garden.

"You can see how our business and grounds tie together," Sharon continues. "It makes a nice presentation for customers to come to the shop and look at the pieces, the colors, the finishes, then have a little bit of a tour to see what the piece looks like in a landscape setting." Although they are often consulted by professional designers, the Lawlesses have created their own landscape plan and have done all the laborious digging and planting themselves. The workshop and display room are in the same Japanese style as the house, a style that fits well into the setting of branching conifers and Zen-like expanses of granite.

Combining work and art makes for a very satisfying life, Sharon says. "I certainly have been making the garden a lot more beautiful than I probably would have if we didn't have the business," she admits. "We've done all the

KEVIN SHIELDS

Phid Lawless's classically simple Lunaform pots provide the means for gardening on the rock ledges of the Quarry Garden.

Old granite quarries inevitably fill with water, providing a perfect backdrop for the Japanese-style house.

KEVIN SHIELDS

landscaping, all the rock walls. This was just a big rubble pile. We fished stuff out to make the pool and used it to level the driveway." The drive borders the largest pool, dividing the house from its mirrored reflection. Granite terraces slide down into the water like smooth stone "beaches." Chunks of cut stone are small islands, and planters full of flowers find natural niches and platforms at various levels. Another water-filled quarry pond is home to Sharon's pink water lilies.

All of this gratuitous architecture is what the stonecutters left behind and the Lawlesses unearthed to prodigious advantage. "That was the intention," Sharon says. "We tried not to make a lot of impact on the environment, just work with it, leave everything wild." Nature seems to have been as creative in reclaiming the now-abandoned human intrusion as in establishing the original terrain. The clumps of birch and spruce and juniper that appear to

be deliberately planted for the best effect were already there, growing inexorably out of cracks in the granite, Sharon notes. She and Phid have built stone walls around those which needed protection and used others as the perfect foil for a large jar or a contrasting ground cover. One little side quarry has become a detached outdoor living room backed with a retaining wall of giant stone steps, perfect shelves for huge pots of purple petunias.

Nowhere are the practical and the aesthetic more ingeniously combined than in the kitchen garden, four four- by eight-foot raised beds located on the shallow terraces of an old quarry amphitheater. Designed to make the most of Maine's quirky climate, they provide the Lawlesses with an abundance of salad greens, tomatoes, cucumbers, peas, beans, cabbage, broccoli, and all kinds of herbs. Phid reckoned with plentiful spring rains, possible summer drought—or the reverse. The sixteen-inch cobblestone walls, invisibly mortared on the inside, are built directly on bedrock. An eight-inch wall of stucco-covered concrete caps the stones for a smooth, contrasting finish. At the bottom of each bed is an I-shaped grid of perforated four-inch plastic pipe with a vertical pipe in the center that reaches to the top level of the soil. The ends of each arm drain through holes at the bottom of the stone wall, drying out soggy spring soil for early planting. The bed can be watered evenly through the central pipe, and the drain holes can be plugged in dry weather to preserve moisture. The inside of the bed is sealed with a cement-based waterproof sealer. Like his planters, which make flower gardening possible in unlikely terrain, Phid's raised beds make growing vegetables an equally viable option.

Sharon confines her on-the-ground gardening to several little shallow beds where lavender and herbs and a few perennials thrive

The Grand Masters of Maine Gardening

*Sharon's artfully placed container plants complement the hardy native species that scratch
a living in the natural basins and cracks of the granite.*

Bare Ledge Blossoms for Phid and Sharon Lawless

with plenty of watering. She can always dip her watering can into a handy pool. "I have no formal training in garden design, but I'm passionate about flowers in my planters," she says. She learned about gardening by just going to greenhouses and looking for plants with a variety of colors and textures, different sun and shade preferences. One planter contains a cascading pink fairy rose, entwined with pink mandevilla, oregano, and scented thyme. "I use a lot of herbs in my planters. I like everything to be free and loose," Sharon explains. "I always look for things I don't have to deadhead a lot, too. I have a few petunias [whose spent blossoms need to be picked off regularly to prolong bloom], and every year I tell myself I'm never going to buy another petunia as long as I live, but I always get sucked in anyway." True, quite a few petunias have captivated her: purple petunias in a terra-cotta urn against gray stones and tree trunks in a dark nook; magenta petunias and white browallia in an upthrust gray cone strikingly poised beside a granite pyramid that echoes the pot's shape in reverse; white petunias tumbling with blue

"I use a lot of herbs in my planters. I like everything to be free and loose."

catmint from a low planter in a sunny spot. Sharon faithfully deadheads every planter in the garden every day.

The fairy rose and the mandevilla, perennials in warmer climates, Sharon treats as annuals. In fact, she can use only annuals in the planters, since even tough perennials cannot survive winter in pots above ground. But the pots themselves are winter-hardy because of their materials and construction methods. "If you keep the container full of soil to within half an inch of the top, it survives the winter very well," she says. There's a drain hole in the bottom, and lids are available for the pots but aren't necessary. Every spring Sharon removes the top third of the soil in each pot and adds fresh potting soil before planting. Regular feeding and watering are all that are required, she says.

Planters overlooked on the walk up the road are pleasant surprises on the way back. "This is a replica of a Frank Lloyd Wright piece," Sharon says, pointing to one in a sheltered corner whose rectangular lines contrast sharply with the curves of most of the others. "It can be very contemporary or period Arts and Crafts, depending on where you put it." Unquestionably, Lunaform pots would look wonderful in just about any place of a scale sufficient to their eloquence, but it would be hard to find another setting quite as magnificent as the Quarry Garden that inspired them.

Lupines on the Front Lawn, Birds in the Bush

The Owens' lawn full of lupines continues to flourish nine years after I visited them. Their involvement with wild flora and fauna and their dedication to Baxter State Park only grow deeper. Bucky Owen was on leave of absence from the University of Maine while he served as Commissioner of Inland Fisheries and Wildlife under Governor John McKernan. Upon being reappointed to the position by Governor Angus King, Owen took early retirement from the university to serve four more years as commissioner. He now devotes full time to conservation projects. He is on the board of the Maine chapter of The Nature Conservancy and has just ended a five-year term as U.S. Commissioner of the North Atlantic Salmon Organization.

Imagine a sea of lupines—blues pale and deep, pinks, mauves, lavenders, a pastel panorama as ravishing as any Monet created at Giverny—only a quarter of a mile from downtown Orono. This breathtaking display is only the most spectacular chapter in a year-long text on the management of a natural ecosystem, every page of which is as fascinating, if not always quite as colorful, as lupines in June.

On a little more than an acre, Ray Bucklin "Bucky" Owen and his wife, Sue, practice what Owen has been preaching for twenty-five years as a wildlife biologist on the faculty of the University of Maine. Less obvious than the irrepressible lupines, but more important in the Owens' scheme, is the wide diversity of trees and shrubs that surround them. "Our goal is to see how many different species of plants and birds we can have here," Owen says. To attract them, the couple has nurtured existing species and planted others to create mini-ecosystems. "Birds are what we're primarily concentrating on. In the fall they come in waves to feed, there are so many seeds. It's

really fun," says Owen, whose enthusiasm for the natural world and the State of Maine seems to spill over into every aspect of his life. He keeps no formal bird list, but along with a full range of the more familiar species, he reports hundreds of Bohemian waxwings devouring crab apples in winter, and a bittern that once visited the tiny pond. "We've had kingfishers, a pair of wood ducks, though the pond is too small for ducks. The occasional woodcock and snipe drop in. I see raccoon prints every morning. They come for the frogs." The frog population is so dense that the Owens have been known to shut the windows against their spring night chorusing.

The Owens began developing their wildlife sanctuary ten years ago on a lot they'd long been eyeing because of its south-facing slope and its location close to the university. There were big white pines and the usual assortment of smaller trees on overgrown farmland, the remnants of an orchard—and lupines in the open field. Some of the pines were cut to accommodate the passive solar house they designed, set into the hillside for energy conservation. Putting that together with the cider they make from the old apples inspired their place's whimsical name, In-Cider Hill.

When the house was built, the lupines' habitat was disturbed. "We have been kind of managing it so the lupine would come back, and they've come back, as you can see!" Owen says. The lupines now cover three-quarters of an acre. It took some experimenting, though. Burning, a common field maintenance practice in Maine, wasn't working. Owen now uses a big rotary mower on the lupine meadow in late July. Midsummer wildflowers take their place—Queen Anne's lace, Indian paintbrush, intensely fragrant Indian hemp (dogbane), milkweed and its attendant butterflies, daisies, lots of vetch. Later come asters and goldenrod.

Lupines pop their seeds when the pods are ripe and come up everywhere, but Owen says that people who want to start a lupine patch have better luck transplanting the roots than scattering seeds. A few years ago the Owens tried planting a wildflower meadow, using Vermont wildflower seeds, but despite extensive tilling and even a light load of herbicide, the aggressive lupines took over every time.

The depth of Owen's dedication is illustrated by one of his first imports to the property, a generous planting of *Amelanchier*, the shadbush that whitens Maine roadsides every spring before the wild cherry blooms. "Its fruits are some of the most nutritious, the most sought after by birds," he points out. "Traditionally, Maine farm homes used to have *Amelanchier*s at their front doors." Another bird staple is the hawthorn. Migrating robins favor it in the fall and survive early spring snowstorms on the fruits that have hung on all

"Shadbush fruits are some of the most nutritious, the most sought after by birds."

winter. Robins make their first nest in the cover of softwoods, such as the hemlock and cedar that Owen planted as a buffer along the road, and raise their second brood in hardwoods after the leaves come out. He's also put in other fruit-bearing shrubs: red osier and silky dogwood, and several varieties of viburnum, including highbush cranberry, the last "overrated" as a bird attraction, Owen says. A white oak he planted bore its first acorns last year.

Where the white pines were thinned, a new growth of hardwoods has sprung up, either brought in by birds or from seeds lying dormant in the ground. "I've selectively cut to create maximum diversity there," Owen says. "Beech, red oak, white oak, sugar maple, white ash, mountain ash, white birch, chokecherry, pin cherry, black cherry, all ones I didn't put in." There is at least one species of shrub that Owen is trying to eradicate, the invasive buckthorn. "It's a cathartic for the birds. They don't eat it unless they're literally starving to death."

Accommodations for birds include houses for bluebirds and swallows, strategically spaced according to the birds' territorial requirements among the old apple trees along the edge of a neighbor's more open land. "These are just about minimum distance for swallows," Owen says. "That one is a bit closer. As such, the swallows won't use it. It's programmed for bluebirds. I hope they come." Flying squirrels like the birdhouses, too. Owen has found their winter nests of moss and cedar bark stuffed into his swallow houses.

Every inch of what Owen likes to call "Noah's Little Acre" is dedicated to the preservation, propagation, or observation of some kind of wildlife. Bird feeders, except for those offering thistle seed, can be kept full only after marauding raccoons den up for the winter. Deer are frequent visitors, coming down at night from the Orono Land Trust property that abuts a corner of the next yard. Moose have looked into the Owens' living room windows.

"We have the highest density of brown and white field mice in Orono," Owen says with a biologist's knowing grin. "Some of the neighbors aren't too keen on the way we manage our yard, with all that tall grass." The only bow to suburban standards is a tiny patch of lawn and a sunny terrace in front of the two-story front windows, where honeysuckle and a flamboyant red trumpet vine cater to hummingbirds. Elsewhere, piles of brush are left to shelter wintering sparrows, and miniature wildflower habitats thrive among small thickets of conifers, wild cherry hedges, and hardwood "forests." One such habitat harbors spring wildflowers—mayapple, Solomon's seal, bloodroot, various ferns, jack-in-the-pulpit, trilliums in white, red, and a rare green. Sheltering under hobblebush and viburnum is a "northern hardwood wildflower garden," dedicated to bunchberry, sarsaparilla, lady's slipper, Indian cucumber root, bluebead lily, and their ilk. Rattlesnake plantain, an orchid with distinctive checkered leaves, thrives in the acid soil under hemlock and tamarack, where Owen plans to develop a "coniferous wild garden." Along the pond grows fireweed, the bright rose-magenta flower that flourishes on burns and roadsides. Wild roses and tall meadowsweet ramble on a bank. Canada lilies "cascade all over the place," as Owen puts it.

Not everything is wild. The Owens have planted a little orchard with Yellow Delicious, McIntosh, and Northern Spy apples, and

RAND RAABE

One of Bucky Owen's woodland habitat areas harbors spring flowers such as red trillium.

cherries and pears. A volunteer apple tree is being used to practice grafting. "I've made nine grafts, and one took. But that's okay," Owen says cheerfully. "I'm learning!" A small vegetable garden has been Sue's project, along with more than her usual share of the other gardening, while Bucky did his stint in Augusta. He laughs when asked how his home wildlife sanctuary fit in with his service as commissioner. "It took my mind off the job," he says. "It fits in more with my ecological background at the university. It's a really nice way to make yards compatible with wildlife, so I think it fits in with respect to state wildlife, too. I'd encourage anybody to do it." He knows a number of people who have created backyard wildlife habitat following his and Sue's example.

About his first fourteen months as Commissioner of Inland Fisheries and Wildlife under Governor John McKernan, Owen is characteristically enthusiastic. Of the six projects he had in mind, one has been a big success and several others got off the ground. He's proudest of the conservation education program for middle-school kids. Funded by both public and private sources, the program sent 240 kids to conservation camp in Bryant Pond for a week last summer, and Owen expects to have five hundred or more this coming summer. "My goal is to see somewhere between eight hundred and a thousand able to go to conservation camp. It introduces them to all aspects of wildlife—fisheries, forestry, orienteering, water safety—those kinds of things." Owen also began a big fisheries initiative to increase the quality of fishing in Maine, to aid the rural economy through building the guiding and sporting camp industries, and to maintain the genetic material of wild brook trout, lake trout, and landlocked

KEVIN SHIELDS

Although the lupines may dominate at certain times, numerous other meadow wildflowers thrive in the Owens' amazingly diversified backyard wildlife sanctuary.

The Grand Masters of Maine Gardening

salmon. "I really enjoyed the job," he says of his days at the Department of Inland Fisheries and Wildlife. "It's a wonderful department, really great people who are very supportive."

Back at home now, Owen can devote more time to his own projects and hobbies, all of them related to the outdoors. He and Sue are avid skiers. Their cross-country skis sit right by the back door. Their trail is the path they keep mowed for hikers and skiers that leads from the road, across their yard to the Orono Land Trust acreage. "I'm a great believer in common land," Owen says. "Everybody knows they are perfectly welcome." The forty-four-acre land trust property was the last piece of open ground between two residential streets. When word got out it was going to be developed, everyone in the neighborhood got together and raised close to fifty thousand dollars to buy it, money that was matched by a federal grant.

When time permits, the Owens ski farther afield. "For eighteen years now, we've spent New Year's Eve somewhere in Baxter State Park," Owen relates. Their son and daughter, now pursuing adult lives that include plenty of time in the outdoors, were about ten and twelve when they first began that tradition. The Owens have invited other family members to join them on these winter ski trips. "Our claim to fame is that no one has ever come twice," Owen says with a laugh. Baxter State Park is their favorite spot on earth, they say. As head of Inland Fisheries and Wildlife, Owen was one of three commis-

sioners for the park, "so it comes right back home," he says. "I've been on the advisory committee for a number of years. We're really enthusiastic about what goes on up there." He has also served on the Land Use Regulation Commission.

The Owens are looking forward to a sabbatical in a couple of years, which they hope to spend in Central America. Owen has been vice president of the Maine Chapter of The Nature Conservancy, which has worked with nongovernmental conservation organizations in South and Central America, an area he has never visited, although he has spent time with students in Africa. "Because I teach policy, and it's the international area I'm weakest on, I figure I should go right down there and get into the middle of it." He hopes to gain new knowledge that will supplement his work with students who want to combine international issues with wildlife management.

Bucky Owen, a native of Rhode Island, came to Maine to attend Bowdoin College. Later, while finishing up his doctorate in zoology at the University of Illinois, he was weighing the possibility of going to Maine or Alaska. Maine's offer came first. "I'm on my way" was his answer. Bucky and Sue Owen have just finished their twenty-seventh year here. "We love the state. You couldn't move us with a shoehorn," he says. "The wildlife program at the university is top-notch. It ranks right up there nationally." And Orono is a great place for growing lupines.

Doc Pinfold's Daffodils—and Lupines

Russ and Jean Pinfold are still visiting their daffodils on Mere Point, still enjoying the gardens Russ planted around their Topsham home and the comfort and sociability of retirement. Nearing ninety, Russ for years stood slightly in awe of his fellow gardener across the bay, the late Currier McEwen.

For some twenty-five years now, several thousand daffodils have been dancing in the April breeze against the superb backdrop of sparkling blue water and the spruce-lined Harpswell shore beyond. Dr. Russell Pinfold, a local veterinarian as legendary in midcoast Maine as James Herriot was in Yorkshire, naturalized them on the secluded property where he and his wife, Jean, built a home at a quiet distance from his busy clinic on Brunswick's outer Maine Street.

"We moved down there for the serenity and beauty," says Pinfold, now eighty-four, who commuted the few miles up the road for a dozen years before retiring in 1984. "I was perfectly willing to come back to the office at night on emergency calls, even though it was a little more effort than walking from the house [next door] to the hospital. It was better for the whole family." Two years ago the Pinfolds, no longer wanting to cope with the upkeep of the property and the relative isolation, decided to sell and move to a retirement community in nearby Topsham. "Luckily," says Pinfold, "we sold to absolutely the right people, which was more important than holding out for the right price. Bob and Ann Hazzard enjoy the flowers and the beauty of it so much. We have a good rapport with them. We're welcome to go down to look at

the flowers, do anything we wish, even weed for them!" he says with a laugh.

"It's still his garden and always will be," says a genial Bob Hazzard. "We enjoy their coming. They've just engaged a couple of caretakers."

The Pinfolds bought the land, a hayfield that was part of an old farm, in the 1950s, when shore property was still affordable. Russ—to his many friends, "Doc" to countless farmers and pet owners he served day and night for thirty-five years—worked on the property in his spare time and started planting bulbs the year before they built their modest "deck house," as he calls it, referring to the decks that provided grandstand seats for garden and wildlife watching.

One of the first things Russ did was to stabilize the bank facing the ocean, a surprising sheer cliff of clay along this mostly rockbound coast. To prevent further erosion of the steep bank, he covered it with waste hay chaff and seed to hold the soil and encourage native grasses, juniper, pussy willows, and young pine trees. Besides preserving his property, his purpose was to deter silting of the clam flats below, exposed at low tide. A dedicated environmentalist who served for fourteen years on the Brunswick Marine Resources Committee, he stresses the importance of maintaining a viable industry for local clam diggers.

"After moving down there," Russ relates, "between office and farm calls, my great pleasure was planting flowers and opening up perennial beds. Nothing was there when we moved. It was an open hayfield that hadn't been cut for years." Though it wasn't necessary to bush hog the field, it first had to be mowed with heavy equipment. For years he gave away the hay, but eventually had to pay to have it cut, a cost he was willing to bear in order to preserve the grassland. "Seeing those waving grasses was important to us. A lot of people would say, 'Why not put it into a tree farm? You can save taxes.' Nonsense!" he snorts. "We went down there for the beauty and quietness. That's about it."

Russ planted between two and three thousand daffodils. A broad swath overlooks the bay. Daffodils and wildflowers, backed by rhododendrons and pine forest, border the four-hundred-foot drive. At its roadside entrance a golden explosion of forsythia welcomes a spring visitor. A little later, blue and white Siberian iris grace the field side of the drive, many of them from the Pinfolds' neighbor across the bay, the renowned hybridizer Dr. Currier McEwen. On a rise behind the house, Pinfold naturalized more drifts of daffodils around a perennial bed that spans the width of the land. "Where Jean's kitchen windows looked out, I would always plant gardens of crocus and daffodils. It eased up housekeeping," he reminisces.

The Hazzards now enjoy Pinfold's thoughtful choreography as the season's show progresses from early perennials to a midsummer extravaganza of daylilies, mallow, daisies, black-eyed Susans, and many more until frost brings down the curtain on a blazing finale of chrysanthemums. Conspic-

KEVIN SHIELDS

Great swaths of daffodils enliven former hay-fields overlooking Merepoint Bay and Birch Island.

uous by their absence are delphiniums, a staple of Maine seaside gardens. Pinfold explains that strong onshore winds wreak havoc with such tall plants, so he made up for their absence with a dazzling display of sturdier lupines, the other early summer mainstay. As he drove around the countryside on farm calls, Pinfold gathered wild lupine. "It's hard to transplant," he acknowledges, "but I figured out how to do it. I collected seeds as well, and finally had the whole slope covered with lupine." Pinfold confided the secret of transplanting wild lupines. "It's essential to find them growing in a spot that's as close a replica of the place where you're going to plant them as possible and to take note of the direction of the sun. That's really important. Because the root is so deep, dig the smaller plants and dig well around them. And be sure to take along some soil to fill the hole. Landowners get mad as hell if you leave holes."

To maintain a dramatic planting of daffodils, replace them when they wear out, advises Doc Pinfold, who also recommends sticking to tried-and-true varieties.

KEVIN SHIELDS

For some reason, Pinfold has never had success with roses, even the rugged rugosas that normally thrive on the coast. Daffodils, however, have responded to his care magnificently. He swears by his recipe: Dig off four inches of topsoil and set it aside, then dig out another four inches of the less fertile subsoil. Return topsoil to the bottom of the bed, set the bulbs in it, and add "a good dollop of bone meal." Refill the bed halfway and soak it well, then return the rest of the soil and soak it again and water regularly. The soaking, and planting in September, earlier than is usually recommended, ensure good root growth before winter, he says. He also found that preparing new beds for fall planting in spring, when the ground is easily workable, is preferable to trying to till up summer-toughened soil later.

Pinfold dismisses the popular notion that raccoons and skunks dig up the bulbs and eat them. "They do not," he says emphatically. "Where the soil is broken, they dig in it to get the worms." To prevent their bothersome excavations, he would lay logs over the plantings and take them up in a few weeks, after the ground settled. Careful observation also convinced him that squirrels and chipmunks are not responsible for the disappearance of fall-planted bulbs. "Last year I helped a neighbor plant a hundred and fifty big, healthy bulbs. They never came up. I dug them up, and they were all mushy. The animals did not dig them up and eat them." Many people had the same experience in the spring of 1997. Pinfold thinks it must have had something to do with the odd winter. Deer will eat tulips, but not daffodils, he notes, so he never bothered to plant tulips.

To maintain a dramatic planting of daffodils, Pinfold advises, "When they wear out, don't try to replant them. Replace them. And stick to the basic varieties—'King Alfred',

The Grand Masters of Maine Gardening

'Mount Hood', 'Ice Follies', 'Lady Backhouse' ['Mrs. R. O. Backhouse']—the solid ones. You can get bloom from April right up to early June. There are some gorgeous daffodils, if you want to specialize in exotic ones, but mine were all those that could withstand a rough climate." He didn't feed them with any of the special bulb fertilizers, nothing but "good old-fashioned steamed bone meal. The secret of masses of daffodils," he says, "is, don't mow them till the leaves turn brown. Just let the grass grow till sometime in July, when the leaves start to turn brown, then mow it down." But even naturalized bulbs don't go on forever. "When they get too crowded or too small, it's cheaper to replace them. If I see they're wearing out, I dig up a spot, put in big, healthy bulbs, and let 'er rip," he declares.

Pinfold dismisses the popular notion that raccoons and skunks dig up the bulbs and eat them.

For growing things, there's nothing better than plenty of cow manure, Pinfold believes. "Someone asked me once why I didn't have a better station wagon. I said that when I was out on farm calls, I had to be able to lug home a couple of bushels of manure whenever I felt like it." An adamant supporter of organic methods, Pinfold used to have two compost bins going all the time. "I wouldn't think of not composting," he says. "People say you shouldn't put things like orange peels into your compost. Baloney! I put in everything— grapefruit, bananas, everything but meat scraps." He has never used pesticides or herbicides. "If you mow your lawn correctly— about two inches high—you don't need all those weed killers or fertilizers." Pinfold spent so much time on all fours, digging and weeding, that one of his sons once told him, "You know, Dad, if there's ever a hereafter, I think you'll come back as a groundhog."

The Pinfolds have exchanged the expanse of gardens, woods, and fields—and work—of their seaside home for the comfort and community of congregate living at The Highlands, in Topsham, but with a few compromises. Instead of the calls of seabirds and the activity of the foxes, deer, and otters, they can hear children playing in the nearby schoolyard. Instead of the drudgery of doctoring large animals—"The horses were kicking harder, the calves were stuck tighter," Russ recalls succinctly—he can walk over to the racetrack at the Topsham Fairgrounds, where he can smell the horses and hobnob with their owners. (And pick up a bucket or two of horse manure for the few beds of annuals—no bulbs—he planted around his new home.)

"Look at this place, what I've done so quickly with just some good horse manure," he says. He satisfies his love for gardening without the work by serving on the retirement community's landscaping committee. "This is such a nice place to live. If you say you'd like to do this or that [around the grounds], they say, help yourself." A lifelong supporter of education, Pinfold can go over to the school and talk to classes about his travels or encourage girls to follow his profession. "I have the best of two worlds," he declares with undiminished enthusiasm.

A Gardening Heritage Lives On in Kezar Falls

Of all the master gardeners, their disciples, and their wonderful gardens, none are as truly representative of the two-hundred-year-old lineage of Maine gardeners as Rhonda Wedgewood and Rick Sanborn. As always, they're hard at work expanding and refining what is an authentic, if giant-size, cottage garden—"anything you really love, with no constraints." The waterfall and brook described in this 2001 article have been completed, and a new addition is an outdoor railroad. Rhonda and Rick have also gotten married.

All my peonies came from both my grandmothers," says Rhonda Wedgewood proudly. So did many of her roses and lilacs. And that's only the beginning. A good two-thirds of the bounteous bloom that surrounds her hilltop home in Kezar Falls originated with family, neighbors, and friends. "One of my grandmothers lived in the farmhouse right around the corner. The other grandmother lives [nearby] in the village. They're all local folks," Wedgewood explains. Her home and garden enjoy a choice site in the former apple orchard of her grandfather, Lawrence Stacey. "He thought this would be the best place for me to build, so he gave us the land. We [Rhonda and her first husband] built here twenty-six years ago. I played here in the apple trees when I was a little girl. When I was digging gardens I got into apple tree stumps. That was kind of neat."

The farm was Elm Row Dairy, run by her grandfather and his brother, Clarence, who supplied milk throughout the Kezar Falls area. They also made maple syrup. The dairy business (and the row of elms) gone, Wedgewood's father, Rodney Stacey, now produces Stacey Farms Maple Syrup at the farm, which has

been in the family for five generations. Her other grandfather was Carl Hammond, a well-known watchmaker in Kezar Falls. Wedgewood's business partner, good friend, and fellow gardener, Rick Sanborn, is from Baldwin, where "the largest pine tree ever cut in Maine" stood on his grandfather's land.

Upon this firm foundation of family and community heritage, Yankee ingenuity and independence, Rhonda Wedgewood began building her garden twenty-six years ago. She hauled flat rocks from an old lead mine over in a corner of the farmland to make steps. Material for the long stone wall along the back of the garden, with its incomparable vista of the Ossippee River Valley and the foothills of the White Mountains, came from ledge blasted for the house's foundation. "All these rocks . . . and what was I going to do with them? So, not knowing what I was doing, I just started stacking them on the original base [of the old cow pasture wall]. When you stand at one end, it looks kind of like a snake. It looks like the old-timers' did, better than a straight one. My daughter's twenty-six now, and she was on my back in a backpack [as I worked]. I never rebuilt it."

Wedgewood dug up the splendid white

birches now bordering her front lawn when they were just black-barked saplings out in the family woodlot. Her hemlock hedges also started as small fledglings from the forest. She laughs as she explains the mountain ash in the center of her lawn. She wanted a maple and thought she'd dug one up in the woods. When it finally leafed out, she realized her mistake. "And it wasn't even the kind with the orange berries!" The lady's slippers, trilliums, and jack-in-the-pulpits, and the pines they grow under, also came from her own property. For her flagpole, she "went up in the woods, cut down a pine tree, left it lying in the sun for a couple of hours. Then you can peel the bark off just like a banana." She built the white picket fence that surrounds the swimming pool, its graceful, scalloped profile a mirror of the distant mountain ranges. She had time on her hands one evening and decided to tackle the rustic fence out front that sets off a favorite rose. "When I was putting it together, I couldn't see much in the dark. I measured wrong. I've got to fix it," she relates amiably.

Among all these semipermanent fixtures (they're always getting moved around at the mercy of some new inspiration) flourishes a prodigious variety of shrubs and flowers, offspring of long-ago contributions, each with a history. "A lot of plants, when I first started, came from different older people in town. They knew I was gardening and they would always give me stuff," Wedgewood continues. "That yucca plant came from my grandmother's lawn. I didn't know what it was. I never saw it do anything, just thought it was different. The year after I put it in, she died. It's [been blooming] ever since. That was a neat surprise." Pink old-fashioned roses, started as small slips from both grandmothers, sprawl over a low wall along the roadside. "There's no maintenance. They just grow," says Wedge-

A pair of Adirondack chairs await one of the rare moments when avid gardeners Rhonda Wedgewood and Rick Sanborn take a minute to rest.

wood. "I've never sprayed them, never fertilized. They come up everywhere. I have one down by the pool. The birds dropped the seed and it just started growing. It's huge now."

Roses are ubiquitous, and many of them are summer-long bloomers. One vigorous specimen was "just a little shoot last year. My son and his wife gave it to me for Mother's Day because they wanted me to have a plant in my garden from them," says Wedgewood with a warm smile. A sheltered spot is devoted to tea roses, which survive according to instructions that came with them from Old Sheep Meadows Nursery in Alfred. The Grubers "have been doing it for forty years," says Rick Sanborn. "We mulch the roses to about a foot above where the growth starts."

He points with a history-lover's pride to another planting. "These irises came over from England in the 1800s. They came from friends of my family, who lived in the third

Rhonda estimates that two-thirds of the plants in her heirloom garden came from family and friends.

house ever built in Baldwin." Sanborn started his gardening hobby when he worked for that family as a seventh-grader, watering seedlings in their greenhouse. Wedgewood has planted and divided the irises again and again. In addition to these English irises, a pale blue complement to a backdrop of roses, she has forty different kinds of "great big giant" bearded irises, Japanese irises, and Oriental and Asiatic lilies of every hue. Where lupines, some with eighteen-inch flower spikes, bloom in June, daylilies take over in summer. While some of them came from a grower in Porter who boasts a hundred and fifty varieties, others, not surprisingly, came from Wedgewood's sister and sister-in-law.

Her hollyhocks are a legacy from her Grandfather Hammond. "When I was a little girl, he wanted to have hollyhocks. He went to a friend's house, dug some up, and just kept fertilizing them. He has pictures of me standing beside them when they were twice as tall as I was." Their descendants are just as spectacular. And then there's the huge hibiscus, a remembrance rather than an inheritance. "My grandmother had those growing right beside her farmhouse door. I knew you could get the type that would live through the winter, and I finally found a place that did have them. It was either at Broadway Gardens in South Portland or Plainview Farm in North Yarmouth." Phlox from a grandmother's garden, a zinnia plot because "when I was a little girl, my mother always had a zinnia garden," native pond lilies from a grandfather's pond—all are treasured components of this nostalgic scene. One of her two little ponds is two and a half feet deep in the center. "I never take the lilies out in winter. I just leave them, and they come up every spring. I have a frog who lives in this pond, and it's deep enough for him to hibernate," she says.

Wedgewood is especially fond of her miniature garden. Surrounding a diminutive pool are tiny versions of everything from astilbe to zinnias, carnations, delphinium, roses, petunias, poppies, potentilla, even a miniature gazing ball, a birdhouse, and a baby shoe spilling miniature hens and chickens. The latest landscaping project is another whole garden room, reclaimed from a hayfield. Daylilies in front of a rustic fence border the lawn, and in one corner a new rock garden surrounds a pool fed by a waterfall, all the work of a couple of weekends by the indefatigable Wedgewood-Sanborn team.

Given Maine's geology, a rock garden was inevitable, and not just because Wedgewood, like her ancestors, had to put rocks somewhere when she was making lawns. "I just put them in the gardens." But her rock garden is more cosmopolitan than that. "I have all kinds of special rocks," she says. "Every time I turn around, Rick has put something else on my wall or in a garden—amethyst, rose quartz, mica, all kinds of crystals."

"It's a little fancier rock garden than most," Sanborn explains, "because we have the gem and mineral and jewelry shop [The Village Jeweler in Cornish]. We work all those gems and minerals right into the gardens. I like tying the rocks and minerals together with gardening."

"Nature is so remarkable," Wedgewood adds thoughtfully. She and Sanborn belong to the Portland Mineral Club, which gives them access to many of Maine's mines not open to the public. When the couple are not gardening, they're often out rockhounding for fun. For their business, they buy most of their gemstones from local miners, then design and set them themselves.

Such a multitude of plant material, set among so many other Maine accents—rocks,

Western Maine's foothills are the backdrop for the hilltop farm where Rhonda's grandfather once raised dairy cattle and apples.

stone walls, fences, old millstones, and wagon wheels—may seem overwhelming, but the sheer exuberance of growth, the unquestionable health and vigor of every specimen, and the unbounded enthusiasm of the gardeners make a visit to this garden a pure delight. Both have deep roots in western Maine, take pleasure in family history, and find it hard to pass by an antique shop or a flea market. "The house is not old, but everything inside is sentimental," says Wedgewood. At the same time, they live by that essential dynamic for honoring tradition—turning ancestral energy into new creativity.

What could be a more living tribute to the past than an ever-evolving garden?

KEVIN SHIELDS

Appendix
Nurseries and Gardens Open to the Public

THE McLAUGHLIN GARDEN AND
HORTICULTURAL CENTER, 97 Main Street,
South Paris, Maine (P.O. Box 16, South
Paris, Maine 04281); 207-743-8820;
fax 207-734-3977; www.mclaughlingarden.org

THE ASTICOU AZALEA GARDEN, at the
junction of Routes 3 and 198, in Northeast
Harbor, Maine, is open to the public from
dawn to dusk, May 1 to November 1.
Entrance and visitor parking on Route 198
near intersection with Route 3.

THUYA GARDEN, on Route 3 in Northeast
Harbor, Maine, is open to the public, free
of charge, from July through September,
7 A.M. to 7 P.M.

CELIA THAXTER'S GARDEN, Appledore
Island, is open Wednesdays from the
beginning of June to the end of August.
For information and reservations, contact
Shoals Marine Laboratory, 607-254-2900
or 607-255-3717; www.sml.cornell.edu

THE MAINE COTTAGE GARDEN, 6 Dodge
Corner Road, Strong, Maine 04983;
207-684-3400; www.mainecottagegarden.com

OLD SHEEP MEADOWS NURSERY,
90 Federal Street, Alfred, Maine 04002
is open 7 days a week, 10 A.M. to 5 P.M.
in season; 207-324-5211;
www.oldsheepmeadowsnursery.com

NORTH CREEK FARM, Route 217,
Phippsburg, Maine 04562; 207-389-1341

YORK'S HARDY RHODODENDRONS,
77 Ridge Road, Bath, Maine 04530;
207-443-5865; yorksrhodys@clinic.net
From April 15 to July 1, open Wednesday
through Monday, 8 A.M. to 6 A.M. From July 2
to November 1, open Friday through Monday,
9 A.M. to 5 P.M.

HARVEY BUTLER MEMORIAL RHODODEN-
DRON SANCTUARY, Springvale, Maine;
Maine Chapter of the New England
Wild Flower Society at the Pine Tree State
Arboretum, P.O. Box 5508, Augusta, Maine;
207-621-0038.

FERNWOOD NURSERY AND GARDENS,
433 Cross Road, Swanville, Maine
(RR 3, Box 928, Swanville, Maine 04915);
fernwood@acadia.net

LUNAFORM, P.O. Box 189, West Sullivan,
Maine 04664; 207-442-0923;
www.lunaform.com

RAND RAABE